PERGAMON INSTITUTE OF ENGLISH (OXFORD)

Language Teaching Methodology Series

Bring the Lab
Back to Life

Other titles in this series include

Bring the Lab
Back to Life

PHILIP ELY

Pilgrims Publications
Canterbury, England

PERGAMON PRESS

Oxford · New York · Toronto · Sydney · Paris · Frankfurt

U.K.	Pergamon Press Ltd., Headington Hill Hall, Oxford OX3 0BW, England
U.S.A.	Pergamon Press Inc., Maxwell House, Fairview Park, Elmsford, New York 10523, U.S.A.
CANADA	Pergamon Press Canada Ltd., Suite 104, 150 Consumers Road, Willowdale, Ontario M2J 1P9, Canada
AUSTRALIA	Pergamon Press (Aust.) Pty. Ltd., P.O. Box 544, Potts Point, N.S.W. 2011, Australia
FRANCE	Pergamon Press SARL, 24 rue des Ecoles, 75240 Paris, Cedex 05, France
FEDERAL REPUBLIC OF GERMANY	Pergamon Press GmbH, Hammerweg 6, D-6242 Kronberg-Taunus, Federal Republic of Germany

First edition 1984

Library of Congress Cataloging in Publication Data
Ely, Philip.
Bring the lab back to life.
(Language teaching methodology and techniques)
1. English language—Study and teaching—
Foreign speakers—Audio-visual aids. 2. English
language—Study and teaching—Audio-visual aids.
3. Language laboratories. I. Title. II. Series.
PE1128.A2E44 1984   438.3'4   83-23648

British Library Cataloguing in Publication Data
Ely, Philip
Bring the lab back to life.—(Language
teaching methodology series)
1. Language and languages—Study and teaching
2. Language laboratories
I. Title II. Series
407'.8 P53
ISBN 0-08-031087-7

Printed in Great Britain by A. Wheaton & Co. Ltd., Exeter

ACKNOWLEDGEMENTS

Firstly, I would like to thank Mario Rinvolucri for his invaluable suggestions, encouragement and guidance, to whom this book owes its present form, if not its existence.

I would also like to thank the teachers and students at the C.P.L.E., Roubaix, for their very helpful suggestions and comments during the testing of certain activities.

The following books deserve acknowledgement for their role in inspiring certain activities:

Awareness Activities (Christine Frank & Mario Rinvolucri)
Elementary Stories for Reproduction (L. A. Hill)
Intermediate ''   ''   ''
Advanced ''   ''   ''
Listening Links (Marion Geddes & Gill Sturtridge)
Once Upon a Time (John Morgan & Mario Rinvolucri)
Sounds Interesting (Alan Maley & Alan Duff)
Talk English (Plowright)
Know your own Personality (H. J. Eysenck & G. Ford)

The following people deserve credit for other ideas incorporated into some of the activities: Richard Allwright, David Evans, Anne Grzesiak, Joan Hewitt and Judith Sluggett.

Philip Ely

CONTENTS

Introduction   ix

       Who is this book for?
       What does this book offer?
       Can I do these activities in *my* lab?
       What level do my students have to be?

Practical Notes   xiii

    A   The different stages of the activities
    B   Monitoring and correction
    C   Erasing the students' tapes
    D   Dividing the lab up into listening groups
    E   What to do if booths break down
    F   The teacher's voice
    G   Using the lab for 'rehearsals'

Section A: *Activities which involve accurate listening with a simple written or graphic response*   1

    1   How well to you know yourself?   3
    2   General knowledge quiz   9
    3   Mystery drawing   13
    4   What's the hidden message?   15
    5   Fibs or bloody great lies?   19

Section B: *Activities requiring accurate communication of information between students*   25

    6   Mystery objects   27
    7   Make it or draw it   30
    8   My living-room   32
    9   Wanted!   34
    10   You can't miss it!   37
    11   Second-hand news   42
    12   Self-dictation   47
    13   Telephone situations   49
    14   Eavesdropping   53
    15   Three-part stories   64

Section C: *Activities in which the student provides appropriate and spontaneous responses to a series of stimuli*   67

16   Listen! What's going on?   69
17   One-sided telephone dialogues   70
18   Open drills   72
19   Do-it-yourself story kit   77
20   Get out of that!   80
21   Murder at the Manor   83

Unclassified

22   Tell the story your way   98

INTRODUCTION

Who is this book for?

A considerable proportion of today's language teachers, in a variety of different teaching environments, have access to a language laboratory. These machines cost a lot of money. Are they worth it?

This book is for those teachers who have a language laboratory at their disposal and who feel the need to exploit this expensive material far beyond the limits of tediously repetitive drills. It is for those teachers whose students go to the lab dutifully rather than eagerly, to get the exercises over and done with. It is also for those teachers who may already have experimented with putting some life into their lab sessions, and who would welcome more new ideas.

What does this book offer?

The following points summarise the considerations which were kept in view throughout the compilation of this book.

(1)   Why is it that, in many lab situations, human beings are herded into little compartments and turned into parrots? Can't they be allowed to remain human beings? Why should they invariably have to say what their machines want them to?

In all (but one) of the activities in this book requiring some kind or oral response from the students, the response always has a degree of spontaneity. This spontaneity may be complete or guided; in the latter case, the student's response is focused on a given field of vocabulary or around a target structure. The lab-occupants and their responses thereby maintain their individuality, a situation opening up other possibilities which will be clarified later.

(2)   Should we really believe that the nastiest medicine is the best? Although it seems that some efforts have recently been made to sugar that with which some students are regularly dosed, wouldn't it be preferable to find one with an altogether better taste?

While structural, pronunciation and intonation exercises may remain an undeniably important part of language training, the language laboratory also has a vast potential enabling stimulating and enjoyable activities. This book contains a challenging variety of ideas which show how this potential can be exploited.

(3)   Why should students and their booths be like the proverbial Englishmen and their castles? When was the last time your students visited each other's booths?

The isolation of a booth has its advantages and disadvantages. Someone who doesn't speak much in the class might be more forthcoming in the privacy of his or her own booth. On the other hand, it seems to go against the all-sharing aspect of the classroom to deny the students access to each other's efforts. Several of the activities in this book encourage booth-swapping; this may be either as an integral and essential part of an activity involving the accurate communication of information between the students, or simply because the students might be expected to be curious enough to hear what their classmates have been up to.

All the activities in this book involve at least one of the following:

(a)   accurate listening comprehension,

(b)   the accurate communication of comprehensible information,

and   (c)   the giving of appropriate and spontaneous responses (as opposed to 'set' responses).

These are among the faculties tested by the ARELS oral examination, of which several sessions (at three levels of difficulty) are organised each year. The entire examination is recorded on a master tape which is broadcast to the candidates in the booths of a language laboratory. Each candidate's responses to the examination are recorded onto the tape in his or her booth and subsequently sent off to ARELS for assessment.

The activities in this book would be helpful insofar as they would enable potential ARELS candidates to get used to the idea of providing responses which are meaningful, communicative, spontaneous and appropriate. Few 'ordinary' lab drills and exercises, whatever their other merits, cater for these aspects. This book could thus be used to supplement any preparatory work done using the recordings of previous ARELS examinations.

Can I do these activities in my lab?

The activities in this book require only those features which are common to most audio-active-comparative language laboratories, that is to say:

(1)   *A teacher's console* from which all the booths, or selected booths, can be controlled.

(2)   *Any number of student booths* controllable by the students themselves when required.

(3)   *A two-track recording system in the students' booths,* that is to say:

   (a)   A 'teacher' or 'source' track which is recorded from the teacher's console and which the students cannot erase;

   (b)   A 'student' track which is recorded via each student's microphone which he or she can erase when required.

(4) *An intercommunication facility:*
  (a) Private, i.e. teacher and one student;
  (b) General, i.e. teacher and all the students.
Other features which would be useful, but not essential, are as follows:
  (a) *A rapid copying facility.* This would enable you not only to get material recorded quickly onto the student's tapes, but also to erase their tapes quickly for those exercises requiring this (see PRACTICAL NOTES below).
  (b) *A conference facility.* This enables you and your students to converse in the lab without everyone having to take their headphones off and leave their booths. This would be particularly useful during brief phases where you invite corrections to certain mistakes from the whole class (see **Monitoring and correction** below).

What level do my students have to be?
The different activities in this book range from a 'semi-beginner' to an 'advanced' level. The approximate level of each activity is indicated, although in many cases you could adapt the activity to any level simply by substituting appropriate material. It might be added that the author's aim is that this book should provide not only 'off-the-peg' activities, but also templates upon which you can base 'tailor-made' ones.

PRACTICAL NOTES

(A) The different stages of the activities

Each activity is presented in several different parts under the following sub-headings:

Outline:

This gives a brief description of the activity for anyone browsing through the book.

Preparation:

This includes things to be done just before, or well before, the lab part of the activity. Certain parts of *Preparation* are accompanied by exclamation marks: !! indicates essential preparation which should be done well in advance, the day before, for example. This chiefly includes the finding or preparation of specific material required in the activity.

! indicates things which have a bearing on the organisation of the lesson as a whole: the teacher would be advised to make sure, in advance, that he or she can cope with them accordingly. Often included in this category is the pre-teaching of language likely to be useful in the activity, (which some teachers could do 'off-the-cuff' with the help of the vocabulary pages mentioned below), or the pre-recording of material onto the students' tapes before they go to the lab.

Procedure:

This contains step-by-step instructions for the lab part of the activity.

Development:

This outlines a suggestion for a further activity to deepen or reinforce the ideas encountered during the main lab activity.

Reproduction:

Here, some advice and explanation is given as to how to do the activity again at a later date with different material.

Variation:

This suggests another lab activity based on the same theme.

Tapescript:

This of course indicates what is to be found on the accompanying cassette. This is clearly useful in knowing what points, if any, need to be dealt with before the lab part of the activity. The tapescripts could also be copied and given to the students after the activity by way of reference and consolidation.

Vocabulary:
This is simply a list of words or expressions to help the teacher in whatever pre-teaching is done. The lists are often copious, but should not be considered as exhaustive.

(B)   Monitoring and correction

Monitoring by the teacher
Since it is virtually impossible to deal with each individual mistake made in the lab, it would seem preferable, and more productive, to focus your attention (and that of your students) on the kind of mistakes whose correction benefits more than just one person. From your experience you will be familiar with the kind of mistakes that crop up frequently: during an activity, you could listen in discreetly and jot down those you hear. When a convenient moment arises to deal with them, you could write them up on the board and then invite your students to come up and make the necessary alterations themselves (you intervene only when mistakes remain unsatisfactorily corrected). Alternatively, you could switch your lab onto the 'conference' system (i.e. you and all your students can talk to each other via headphones), read each mistake out to the class and invite oral corrections. Ideally, any correction should be carried out at some stage when it is not too late for those concerned to go back and correct, although this depends on how the activity is organised.

Monitoring by the students
In those activities lending themselves to booth-swapping, the students could be encouraged to do their own monitoring and correction of each other's work. One way of doing this is to ask them, when visiting a classmate's booth, to write some kind of comments on a piece of paper to be left in the booth. These comments can be praising as well as corrective, and can be added to (or even contradicted) by subsequent listeners. One visitor might, for example, praise the original occupant's clear pronunciation, while another might jot down something that didn't sound right.
At the end of the activity, each student returns to his or her booth to look at the comments made about his or her work. These comments could subsequently be pooled in the class; the corrective ones would be a useful source of material for a 'troubleshooting' session. You would certainly find yourself dealing with a very mixed bag of points, the kind that you might find difficult to integrate satisfactorily into an ordinary lesson.

(C) Erasing the students' tapes

Several activities in this book require, in advance, the erasure of up to 10 minutes' worth of tape in the students' booths, i.e. the 'teacher' or 'source' track in each booth must be wiped clean of anything previously recorded on it. To achieve this, simply do the same as you would to record an exercise onto the students' tapes via your microphone, but turn your microphone volume down to zero.

Better still, unplug your microphone completely if this is possible, as 'zero volume' in some labs is not absolute zero.

The process is obviously quicker if your lab is equipped with the rapid-copying facility.

Any sound recorded onto the students' tapes via their own microphones during this process will of course be erased as soon as they begin their recordings.

(D) Dividing the lab up into separate listening groups

Some activities require that different material be recorded in different groups of booths (usually 3 groups). This can be achieved in different ways, depending on the kind of lab you have:

> (a) From your console, activate one group of booths at a time, and then record the corresponding material onto that group's tapes only.

or (b) Switch off the 'unconcerned' booths while you are recording onto one group's tapes.

or (c) Record all the material onto all the tapes and then rewind each group's tapes to the right place. Don't forget to tell each student to listen only to the part concerning him or her.

(E) What to do if booths break down

Nothing is more exasperating, for the teacher as well as the students, than discovering in mid-activity that one of the booths hasn't worked properly. Prevention being better than cure, you could get into the habit of recording onto *all* the tapes (including those in vacant booths) and then having a quick testing session to make sure all the occupied booths are working, before embarking on the main activity. A quick repetition exercise could be used for the test, and would enable the students to check to see if both the broadcast material and their own voices have been recorded in their booths.

If any booths aren't working properly, the alternatives are:

> (a) Put the students into other vacant booths.
> (b) If possible, put the defective booths to rights quickly (check for twisted, defective or badly-installed tapes, or badly-adjusted volume controls).
> (c) If no other vacant booths are available, let any boothless students

plug their headphones into their classmates' machines and share the booths (this is possible in some labs). They will at least be able to hear what is going on.

(d) Let any boothless student plug into your console (most consoles have at least one other headphone socket) but make sure his or her voice is not recorded onto the others' tapes.

(F) The teacher's voice

Many teachers, through experience, develop an excellent, well-projected classroom voice. This may well be necessary to cut through the babble of the invariable chatterboxes and reach the furthest ears, but in the lab your students hear you as if you were talking right inside their heads. Clearly, then, the way in which you use your voice in the lab can't be taken too much for granted. A voice that is quiet, calm but firm is probably preferable to a loud, authoritative one which sends everyone fumbling for their volume controls.

(G) Using the lab for 'rehearsals'

Each booth could be used to allow the student to 'rehearse' what he or she is going to say later, either in the lab, or in a subsequent class activity (a role-play or a sketch, for example). The advantages are that the rehearsal is private, and the student can listen to him- or herself to check whether what he or she says sounds acceptable.

Although the students might feel more comfortable if they know that you are not eavesdropping on their rehearsals, you can of course remain available for questions or guidance.

SECTION A

*Activities which involve accurate listening
with a simple written or graphic response*

1. HOW WELL DO YOU KNOW YOURSELF?

Level   Intermediate upwards

Outline

The Students listen to a pre-recorded 'personality test' composed of questions giving yes/no answers. They note their answers and then analyse them using the key.

Preparation

! (1)   There are two 'personality' tests recorded on the cassette:
Test A: 'Are you psychic?'
Test B: 'How extrovert or introvert are you?'
Choose the one you want your students to do (the level of language used in test B is generally higher than in test A).

! (2)   Pre-teach any unknown words or expressions.

! (3)   Record the test you have chosen on the students' tapes, if possible before they actually come to the lab.

Procedure

(1)   When your students are sitting in their booths, tell them that they are going to hear questions which test a certain aspect of their personality. For the moment, don't tell them *which* aspect, but *do* impress upon them that their answers are private and need not necessarily be revealed to anyone else.

(2)   Explain that they are to listen to the questions at their own speed, noting the number of each one and their answer to it as follows:
+   denotes 'yes'
−   denotes 'no'
X   denotes 'I understand but I can't answer'
Also encourage them to ask for help with problems when necessary.

(3)   When they have finished, move them to a place where they can converse.

(4)   Ask them to discuss, as a class or in small groups, what they think the questions were supposed to test, before you actually tell them.

(5)   Now let them analyse their answers using the key (on pages 17–18). You could copy this up on the board. They will now be able to see if they have psychic powers, or how extrovert they are.

(6)   Finally, ask them if they thought the test was a good one: get them to comment on the validity of the questions they remember.

3

Tapescript

Test A: *Are you psychic?*

(1) Are your dreams often quite detailed?

(2) Do you get concerned when someone is late for a rendezvous with you?

(3) Would you rather watch a programme about space-travel than a film about children?

(4) Do you feel a little embarrassed when strangers are over-polite to you?

(5) Do you sometimes daydream instead of concentrating on the work you are doing?

(6) Is your first opinion of people usually favourable?

(7) Can you draw recognisable sketches of things?

(8) Are you generally capable of doing ordinary repairs about the house?

(9) Do distant friends or relatives sometimes arrive or phone when you have just been thinking about them?

(10) Do you have trouble choosing presents for people?

(11) At school, did you prefer mathematics to languages?

(12) Can you sometimes sense that certain places have a bad atmosphere attached to them?

(13) When you're reading a book, do you form a clear picture of the characters in it?

(14) Would you rather visit a car factory than an art gallery?

(15) Do you believe that certain people are telepathic?

(16) Are you sometimes a little inconvenienced when friends call unexpectedly?

(17) Have you ever felt like crying during a particularly moving film?

(18) If you close your eyes, can you form a clear picture of a friend's face?

(19) Do you feel embarrassed when you are alone with someone who doesn't talk much?

(20) Do you know which aspect of your personality these questions test?

Test B: *How extrovert or introvert are you?*
- (1)   Do your friends think you're calm?
- (2)   Do you prefer quiet weekends?
- (3)   Are you sometimes late?
- (4)   Would you prefer reading to doing sport?
- (5)   Do slow drivers irritate you?
- (6)   Are you a busy kind of person?
- (7)   Do you like to be alone from time to time?
- (8)   Do you do your Christmas shopping at the last moment?
- (9)   Would fishing be too boring for you?
- (10)   Do you find it difficult to be polite to some people?
- (11)   Are you at home only rarely?
- (12)   When you meet a friend, are you generally the first to say 'hello'?
- (13)   Do you prefer to know in advance when your friends are going to visit you?
- (14)   Do you walk faster than most people in the street?
- (15)   Do you do a lot of different things in your spare time?
- (16)   Do you think that people who read in the toilet are ridiculous?
- (17)   Do you sometimes feel nervous when the phone rings?
- (18)   Do you sing in the bath from time to time?
- (19)   Do you feel a little embarrassed when you're alone with someone who doesn't talk much?
- (20)   Do you often wish you had more time?
- (21)   Are you a little apprehensive about trying strange foreign dishes?
- (22)   When you're watching a comedy film, do you usually laugh more than the other spectators?
- (23)   Do some people think you're untidy?
- (24)   Do you ever worry about your home when you're away on holiday?
- (25)   If you went into a restaurant and discovered that the service was very slow, would you prefer to get up and leave rather than complain?
- (26)   Do you get excited when watching your favourite sport?
- (27)   When the alarm clock goes off in the morning do you get up more or less straight away?
- (28)   If you were invited out to a big dinner, would you feel uncomfortable if you had to sit between people you didn't know?
- (29)   Do your friends sometimes need your advice?
- (30)   Would you make absolutely certain you had another job before resigning?
- (31)   In a conversation with several people, do you tend to be the one who listens?
- (32)   Have you usually got a good reply to people's criticism of you?

(33) If you saw someone in the street that you thought you'd met before, would you walk past rather than say 'hello' and risk making a fool of yourself?

(34) Do you believe that things done spontaneously are better than things that are planned?

(35) Are you extravagant now and then?

(36) Are you fairly good at telling jokes?

(37) Do you think it's ridiculous to talk to yourself?

(38) If you found that someone had blocked your car by parking badly, would you leave an angry note on his windscreen?

(39) Would you feel nervous about speaking in front of a lot of people, even if you knew them very well?

(40) Do you regard your home as the only place you can relax in?

(41) Have you ever been tempted to try something like parachute-jumping or hang-gliding?

(42) Are you good at telling lies?

(43) When getting in touch with someone you don't know very well, do you prefer to write than to phone?

(44) Do you sometimes jump the traffic lights when you're in a hurry?

(45) If someone does something that makes you angry, do you find it difficult to forget?

(46) If you had to go to war, would you rather be a pilot than a soldier?

(47) When you're in a shop, do you sometimes have the impression that you are at the service of the shop-assistant rather than vice-versa?

(48) Are you inclined to say or do things one day that you regret the next?

(49) If someone pushed into the queue you were standing in, would you feel angry but say nothing?

(50) After making a difficult decision, do you tend to worry about the consequences for some time afterwards?

How well do you know yourself?

Key to the personality tests

Count ONE POINT for each time your answer coincides with those indicated.

Example:	Your Answer	Answer given	
	+	+	= 1 POINT
	−	−	= 1 POINT
	+	−	= 0 POINTS
	−	+	= 0 POINTS
	X	(+ or −)	= ½ POINT

Test A. *Are you psychic?*

(1)	+	(6)	+	(11)	−	(16)	−
(2)	−	(7)	+	(12)	+	(17)	+
(3)	−	(8)	−	(13)	+	(18)	+
(4)	−	(9)	+	(14)	−	(19)	−
(5)	+	(10)	−	(15)	+	(20)	(1 point if you were right!)

What your score represents

0–10:   You are not all psychic; you are very pragmatic, with a tendency to be over-anxious about some things. Your abilities and preferences revolve around things with a degree of exactitude, such as technology and mathematics.

11–15:   You probably have some psychic potential, but this is inhibited by a lack of faith and a rather logical outlook on life in general.

16–20:   You are undoubtedly psychic (you probably knew already). You are a dreamer. Your abilities and preferences are orientated towards artistic things and things with an immeasurable aspect to them. You are a very open-minded person and you seldom worry unduly. You, and other members of your family too, are likely to have had some kind of psychic experience already.

Test B. *How extrovert or introvert are you?*

(1)	+	(11)	−	(21)	+	(31)	+	(41)	−
(2)	+	(12)	−	(22)	−	(32)	−	(42)	−
(3)	−	(13)	+	(23)	−	(33)	+	(43)	+
(4)	+	(14)	−	(24)	+	(34)	−	(44)	−
(5)	−	(15)	−	(25)	+	(35)	−	(45)	+
(6)	−	(16)	+	(26)	−	(36)	−	(46)	−
(7)	+	(17)	+	(27)	+	(37)	+	(47)	+
(8)	−	(18)	−	(28)	+	(38)	−	(48)	−
(9)	−	(19)	+	(29)	−	(39)	+	(49)	+
(10)	−	(20)	−	(30)	+	(40)	+	(50)	+

What your score represents.

Look at the scale below and locate your score on it.

0   10   20   30   40   50

EXTROVERSION   AVERAGE   INTROVERSION

A score to the left indicates extrovert tendencies while a score to the right reveals a more introverted personality. What are the characteristics of such people?

Extrovert people

You are an active type: you like moving about, meeting people and doing a lot of different things. You're not afraid of expressing yourself but you're inclined to take risks, be impulsive and even irresponsible sometimes. You're a very sociable and open person but you tend to live each day as it comes, and do things without considering the consequences.

Introvert people

You're the kind of person who likes to be in peace. You don't mind being on your own, in fact you probably prefer it sometimes, but when you're with friends or colleagues, you tend to be a listener rather than a talker. You have self-control and you rarely do things impulsively or without considering the outcome. You don't believe in taking unnecessary risks. You probably prefer situations involving thinking to those requiring action.

2. GENERAL KNOWLEDGE QUIZ

Level   Lower intermediate upwards

Outline
Thirty general knowledge questions are recorded onto the students' tapes. They listen to them at their own speed and write down their answers. The aim of the exercise is to encourage accurate listening comprehension.

Preparation
! (1)   Record the quiz onto the students' tapes, if possible before they come to the lab. (See **Tapescript** on page 10).

Procedure
  (1)   Let the students listen to the recorded quiz at their own speed and write down their answers.
  (2)   Move the students to a place where they can converse.
  (3)   Invite answers from the class before providing the correct ones (check with the answer list on page 11). Ask each student to ring the number of each question s/he got wrong.
  (4)   Now encourage the students to admit their mistakes, following this kind of pattern:

"I thought *New York* was the capital of the United States".

   "I didn't know that *Greenland* was the largest island in the world".

Development
   The students compile a 'class quiz' in two teams.

Preparation
   None.

Procedure
  (1)   Bring all the students out to the front of the class.
  (2)   Ask them to stand in order of height, the tallest at one end of the line and the shortest at the other.
  (3)   Number them off in twos along the line.
  (4)   Sit the 'ones' in one corner of the class and the 'twos' in the opposite corner, so that the two teams so formed can converse without disturbing or overhearing each other.

(5)   Ask each team to compile a short quiz (about 10–15 questions) for the other team. Each team-member must have a copy of the questions decided upon. *Do not give them any help during this phase.* They must decide on the content of the quiz, and the grammatical accuracy of their questions, *as a team.*

(6)   While they are doing this, write these rules up on the board. Draw their attention to them when you have finished.

RULES OF THE QUIZ

(1)   Each team member must ask a question.

(2)   Each team member must try to answer a question.

(3)   Incorrectly-asked questions give one point to the other team.

(4)   Each team has two chances to answer a question correctly: if the first person answers correctly, his team scores two points; if he fails, and a second person from the same team can answer correctly, the team scores one point.

(5)   If one team cannot supply the correct answer to one of their own questions, the other team scores two points.

(7)   Put the two teams opposite each other and begin the quiz, noting the points scored on the board.

Tapescript

General knowledge quiz
(1)   What's the capital city of the United States?
(2)   Which is the commonest word in spoken English?
(3)   How many teeth should a healthy adult have?
(4)   Neil Armstrong was the first man to do what?
(5)   How long does a normal football match last?
(6)   What did James Watt invent?
(7)   In what year did the Second World War end?
(8)   What's the name of the green substance in plants?
(9)   Which country are the Pyramids in?
(10)   What were piano keys originally made of?
(11)   What's the largest island in the world?
(12)   Who, on average, live longer: men or women?
(13)   Which star is nearest the earth?
(14)   Can you spell the word: 'aggressive'?
(15)   Do most front doors open inwards or outwards?
(16)   What's the longest river in the world?
(17)   Which two chemical elements is pure water composed of?
(18)   Was 1980 a leap year?

(19)   What happens to the pupil of your eye when you move from a well-lit room to a dark room?
(20)   Which number does the Roman numeral 'V' represent?
(21)   What's the colour between orange and green in the rainbow?
(22)   What sort of person would give you a prescription?
(23)   Can you spell the word: 'changeable'?
(24)   What's the next prime number after seven?
(25)   What relation would your father's mother's brother be to you?
(26)   For a normal violinist, would the thickest violin string be on his left or his right when he was playing?
(27)   Who was famous for the theory of relativity?
(28)   What sort of person would use a ball and a racket on a court with a net?
(29)   Which part of the body is the smallest bone in?
(30)   How many questions in this quiz were geographical?

Answers to the quiz
(1)   Washington.
(2)   According to the Guinness Book of Records "I".
(3)   32.
(4)   He was the first man to step on the moon (on the 21st July, 1969).
(5)   90 minutes (plus 15 minutes at half-time).
(6)   The steam engine.
(7)   1945.
(8)   Chlorophyll.
(9)   Egypt.
(10)   Ivory.
(11)   Greenland.
(12)   Women. They live, on average, about 6 years longer.
(13)   The sun.
(14)   AGGRESSIVE.
(15)   Inwards.
(16)   The Nile (4145 miles; 6670 km.) The Amazon is measured to be 4007 miles (6448 km) although the length of both rivers is really only a question of definition
(17)   Hydrogen and Oxygen (H_2O).
(18)   Yes.
(19)   It widens (to let more light into the eye).
(20)   5.
(21)   Yellow. (Red, orange, yellow, green, blue, indigo, violet).
(22)   A doctor.
(23)   CHANGEABLE.
(24)   11.

(25)   Your great-uncle.
(26)   On his left.
(27)   Albert Einstein.
(28)   A tennis player.
(29)   The ear. The stapes is about 3 millimetres long and weighs about 3 milligrammes.
(30).   4. (Questions 1, 9, 11 and 16).

3. MYSTERY DRAWING

Level   Intermediate upwards

Outline
The students follow recorded instructions to draw an object whose identity is only revealed if the instructions are followed precisely.

Preparation
! (1)   Look at the tapescript of 'Mystery drawing' on this page and pre-teach or revise the vocabulary you think that your students will need to understand the recording on the cassette (prepositions, geometrical vocabulary, etc.).

! (2)   Make sure everyone has got a sheet of paper about the same size as a page in this book, and a pen.

Procedure
(1)   Record 'Mystery drawing' (which is on the cassette) onto the students' tapes. (They can be in their booths listening).

(2)   Ask them to listen again at their own pace and follow the instructions stage by stage to draw the object. Explain that they will only recognise it if the instructions are followed carefully.

(3)   When they have finished, ask them to compare their results with each other.

Tapescript
I'm going to explain to you how to draw something in several stages. Listen to each stage carefully before you draw.

Stage 1. First, turn your paper horizontally. In the centre draw a five-centimetre equilateral triangle pointing upwards like a mountain. End of stage 1.

Stage 2. Draw an identical triangle, also pointing upwards, to the left of the first one. Make sure that the bottom right corner of the second triangle just touches the bottom left corner of the first one. Do not, however, draw the base of the second triangle. End of stage 2.

Stage 3. Draw a circle, about one-and-a-half centimetres in diameter, around the point where the two triangles touch. End of stage 3.

Stage 4. Now join the tops of the two triangles with a straight line. End of stage 4.

Stage 5. Draw a circle, about five centimetres in diameter, around the bottom right corner of the first triangle. End of stage 5.

Stage 6. Draw an identical circle around the bottom left corner of the second triangle. End of stage 6.

Stage 7. Can you finish the drawing?

Reproduction

You could make up your own instructions for almost any simple drawing: a house, a robot, a piece of furniture, or even a completely abstract design. It would be advisable to choose something that could be drawn by assembling fairly simple geometrical shapes. Also remember that the instructions should be as unambiguous as possible; the author of such instructions doesn't always see the ambiguities until they have been tried by someone else, so it might be a good idea to try out your mystery drawing on someone before you do it with your students.

4. WHAT'S THE HIDDEN MESSAGE?

Level   Intermediate upwards

Outline
The students listen to a recorded passage. They have a list of clues and must use it to find certain 'target' words in the passage. The target words contain letters (indicated by the clues) which constitute a message. Three such messages are 'hidden' in the passage.

Note: This activity represents a good technique of rendering 'routine' passages or dialogues (even fairly dull ones) much more interesting.

Preparation
!! (1)   Make sure the students each have a copy of the clues on the next page.

Procedure
  (1)   Record the passage onto the students' tapes. (They can be in their booths listening).
  (2)   Ask them to listen to the passage at their own pace and use the clues to find the three hidden messages:
         (A) Grant's profession,
         (B) who cut his brakes and
         (C) why.
         Each clue gives one word. The students write this word in the space provided and then write one of its letters (1st, 2nd, 3rd etc. as indicated) in the box. Suggest that they should not spend too long on one clue.
  (4)   Let this listening phase continue for as long as the students want. Go round and see how they are getting on.
  (5)   (In the class or lab). Invite the weaker students to contribute letters to the clues they solved, and write them up on the board. Now invite the stronger ones to supply the letters to fill up any gaps.

Development
  (1)   Ask the students to suggest how the three 'messages', 'SOLDIER', 'HIS FIANCEE' and 'REVENGE' are linked.
  (2)   Now ask them to write a short story relating the events leading up to those in the passage. (This could be set as homework).

15

Clues to find the Hidden Messages

Each clue gives you one word. Each word can be found in the passage. When
you have found each word, write it in the space provided, then write one of its
letters (as indicated in the clue) in the box. Some clues are synonyms, others are
comprehension questions.

(A)

TO DISCOVER GRANT'S PROFESSION

(1) hit with the sole of the foot:	. . . .	1st letter:	☐
(2) preposition used with (1):	. . . .	1st letter:	☐
(3) allowed (to):	. . . .	1st letter:	☐
(4) travelling at:	. . . .	1st letter:	☐
(5) fragments, small parts:	. . . .	2nd letter:	☐
(6) arrived at:	. . . .	2nd letter:	☐
(7) What was hiding the rocks?	. . . .	2nd letter:	☐

(B)

TO FIND OUT WHO CUT GRANT'S BRAKES

(1) moving very fast:	. . . .	1st letter:	☐
(2) thoughts:	. . . .	2nd letter:	☐
(3) turn:	. . . .	1st letter:	☐
(4) sensed:	. . . .	1st letter:	☐
(5) vibrating:	. . . .	5th letter:	☐
(6) despite the fact that:	. . . .	1st letter:	☐
(7) concealed:	. . . .	last letter:	☐
(8) looking out (for):	. . . .	1st letter:	☐
(9) awful:	. . . .	2nd letter:	☐
(10) What Grant might have broken if he'd jumped:	. . . .	2nd letter:	☐

(C)

TO FIND OUT WHY GRANT'S BRAKES WERE CUT

(1) the colour of the dust:	. . . .	1st letter:	☐
(2) how Grant felt when he realised the car was out of control:	. . . .	2nd letter:	☐
(3) a car or lorry, for example:	. . . .	1st letter:	☐
(4) panorama:	. . . .	last letter:	☐
(5) curve (in the road):	. . . .	3rd letter:	☐
(6) What was paralysed?	. . . .	3rd letter:	☐
(7) What did the jeep lose?	. . . .	3rd letter:	☐

Tapescript Find the Hidden Message

Grant only realised the brakes had been cut when the jeep was already in the bend. He stamped his foot desperately on the pedal but it just touched the floor limply. The jeep was now hurtling towards another bend in the rough dirt-track, the wheels throwing up huge clouds of red dust. Grant knew the hand-brake would be useless. His mind raced. There were only two things he could do: throw himself out and risk breaking his neck, or swing the runaway car off the road to the right and hope that the bushes and small trees would stop him. But he knew that if there were any thicker trees hidden among the rest, he wouldn't have much chance of getting out alive. And if he let the car swing so much as a couple of yards to the left, he would be able to spend the last few seconds of his life admiring the mountain landscape before ending it three hundred feet down. He judged he must have been doing about fifty on a road where only a madman would risk doing more than thirty. He felt every rock and bump slowly shaking the jeep to pieces. It was only a matter of time before he reached a tighter bend or even another vehicle. He desperately scanned the band of vegetation on the right hand side. Although it was far from flat, he could see no thick trees hidden among the scorched grass and bushes. Suddenly, his choice was made for him. There was another cloud of red dust half a mile down the road. He didn't know which direction the other vehicle was going in but he knew that the final result would be the same. Without even checking for trees, he threw the jeep to the right. It bounced over the grass-hidden rocks and plunged into the dense growth — the shock was so violent that Grant didn't know if he was still in the jeep or not.

He woke up with a terrible pain in his shoulder and a leg which he couldn't move. The jeep was a few yards behind him with three wheels in the air.

Reproduction

Outline

You could apply the technique in the preceding exercise to other recorded passages or dialogues you have available, even fairly dull ones.

Preparation

!! (1) Choose a recorded passage or dialogue about the same length as the one above.

!! (2) Decide one one or more 'messages' (one or two words each) having some connection with the recording you have chosen. Try to choose messages with an element of intrigue about them: this will make the discussion and writing phases (Development 1 and 2) more interesting.

!! (3)   Look through the tapescript of the recording and underline the words which contain (in order) the letters of each message. Put a ring round the appropriate letter in each word. Where possible, choose words you would like to draw your students' attention to.

!! (4)   Formulate a list of clues which gives these words. You could use synonyms or comprehension questions, as in the preceding activity.

!! (5)   Make copies of the clue-list for your students, or write them up on the board.

Procedure

As for the preceding activity.

5. FIBS OR BLOODY GREAT LIES?

Level   Intermediate upwards

Outline

The students listen to a series of twenty mini-dialogues. In each dialogue, one of the people is telling a lie. Each student judges the relative 'badness' of the lies and marks a cross for each one on a graph; the height of any cross above the preceding one is proportional to its degree of 'badness'. At the end of the activity, each student has a graph with the line running more or less diagonally upwards. The steepness of this line is a measure of the student's 'censoriousness'; a shallow line would reflect a rather permissive nature. This activity leads into a discussion phase.

Preparation

!! (1)   Make sure there is a copy of the graph on page 21 for each student.

 ! (2)   Record the twenty mini-dialogues onto their tapes, preferably before they come into the lab.

Procedure

(1)   Explain that they are going to hear twenty mini-dialogues and that one of the people in each one is deliberately lying.

(2)   Tell them to judge the relative 'badness' of each lie and to give a score ranging from nought (a perfectly acceptable lie) to four (a downright wicked one). Each lie is marked with a cross on the graph; for example, if they judge that lie 1 scores *3* points, they put a cross *3* spaces above the '1' on the base line. If they award *4* points to lie 2, they mark a cross directly above the '2' on the base line but *4* spaces above the first cross. They continue in this way for the other lies, putting each cross a certain number of spaces above the preceding one. Explain this on the blackboard before they begin the activity.

(3)   Now let them listen to the pre-recorded mini-dialogues at their own pace, and draw their graphs. It might be a good idea to go round and see how they are getting on in case anyone is confused about how to do the graph.

(4)   When they have finished, they should each have a line of crosses running more or less diagonally upwards. Ask them to join up the crosses.

(5)   Now ask them to draw a straight line joining the origin of the graph (the double zero point in the bottom left corner) with the point marked 'A'.

(6) Take the class to a place where they can discuss. Ask them what they think the straight diagonal line represents, and how their line of crosses relates to it. (The straight line could be taken to represent a kind of 'average', although it might be better to consider it only as a guide-line. Students with crosses going well above this line are relatively censorious, while those whose crosses fall well below it are rather permissive).

(7) Ask them to discuss in pairs or small groups which lies they thought were particularly bad. They can also compare and comment on each other's graphs.

Development

You could continue the discussion by bringing up the following questions:

(a) Why do people tell lies?
(b) In what kind of situations do people lie?
(c) When was the last time *you* told a lie?
(d) Was it an innocent one? Or a wicked one?
(e) What sort of lies are acceptable?
(f) Are you a good liar when you need to be?
Why?/Why not?
(g) Can you tell when people are lying to you?
How?
(h) Has anyone ever told you a lie which made you angry?

Still on the same theme, ask the students to think silently for a few moments, and to think of a story (e.g. something which happened to them once) which is either *completely* true or *completely* false. Then ask some of them to tell their stories to the class. Each student may then 'cross-examine' the story-teller (two questions each) to see if his story is feasible. After that, you could take a class vote to see how many people believe the story, before actually asking the storyteller to reveal whether it was true or not.

The mini-dialogues could further be used for a register exercise: play the cassette (in the classroom, if possible) and ask the students to suggest who the speakers are and what kind of situation they are in.

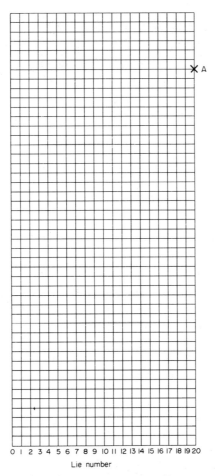

0 1 2 3 4 5 6 7 8 9 10 11 12 13 14 15 16 17 18 19 20

Lie number

Tapescript   Fibs or Bloody Great Lies?

One of the people in each of these dialogues is telling a lie. Be ready to judge how bad you think the lie is in each case.

1.	*Politician:*	We, the Liberal Democrats, will cut income tax by five per-cent! We guarantee zero inflation in two years! We solemnly pledge that the number of unemployed will be down to half a million by the end of the year! We, the Liberal democrats, will put this country on its feet!
2.	*Customs officer:*	Anything to declare? No cigarettes or wine?
	Traveller:	No, no . . .
	Customs officer:	Okay.
3.	*Gang-leader:*	Come on lads! Shall we teach this little twit a lesson?

	Twit:	I wouldn't if I were you. I've got a black belt in karate.
4.	*After-dinner speaker:*	And now I'd like to hand over to Mr. Knowles, who has a few words to say.
	Mr. Knowles:	Well, first of all, let me say how delighted I am to be here with so many distinguished people tonight . . .
5.	*Car-buyer:*	Well, the engine seems okay. Just a little bit of rust here under the doors. Two hundred and fifty pounds . . . hm . . . How old did you say it was?
	Car salesman:	Seven y- er — four years old, yes.
6.	*Boss:*	Jane? Did you remember to call Mr. Sykes?
	Secretary:	Oh, God! Er — yes, Mr Craven.
7.	*Gossip:*	Well! I'd never have believed it!
	Scandalmonger:	Oh, yes! And what's more, he beats his wife!
	Gossip:	(*Gasp!*) Never!!
	Scandalmonger:	Oh, yes! He's a nasty piece of work all right!
8.	*Wife:*	You haven't even noticed!
	Husband:	What?
	Wife:	Well, look!
	Husband:	Oh, yes! You've been to the hairdresser's!
	Wife:	Yes! Well . . . What do you think?
	Husband:	Mmm. Very nice, dear.
9.	*Grandfather:*	So there I was — all alone in the sky — three enemy planes behind me, coming in for the kill!
	Grandson:	Gosh, Grandad, what did you do?
	Grandfather:	Ha ha ha!! I turned round — NNYYAAAGHHH!!! — and shot them all down — all three of 'em! Ha ha ha!! They didn't know what hit 'em!
	Grandson:	Cor!!
10.	*Judge:*	Mrs. Pickering, I'm going to ask you a question. I must ask you to think very carefully about how you answer. What you say is of vital importance in this case. Did you, or did you not, see the accused, Joseph Carton, leave the

		Post Office at ten forty-five on the second of March this year?
	Mrs. Pickering:	Yes, it was him all right. *I* saw him.

11. *Little boy:*   Mum, is Father Christmas really coming tonight?

    Mum: Yes, dear. But he'll only come when you're fast asleep — down the chimney — and he'll put all sorts of things by your bed.

    Little boy: Oooh!

12. *Store detective:*   Excuse me, sir — just one moment. Could you show me what's in your bag?

    Young man: What, this one?

    Store detective: Yes. Have you paid for this?

    Young man: Yes, of course I have!

13. *Store detective:*   Excuse me, sir — just one moment. Could you show me what's in your bag?

    Old man: What, this one?

    Store detective: Yes. Have you paid for this?

    Old man: Yes, of course I have!

14. *Staff manager:*   I see. Well, Mr. Morton, we are looking for someone dynamic, someone with initiative, someone who can make decisions — the right decisions — and make them fast. Tell me, Mr. Morton, do *you* have all these qualities.

    Interviewee: Yes . . . I think so.

15. *Schoolmistress:*   Listen, Tommy. Look at me. Come on, look at me. Was it you that broke that window?

    Tommy: No. miss.

16. *Wife:*   Just think: we've been married five years today. Do you still love me, darling?

    Husband: Yes . . . of course I do!

17. *Guest:*   Mmm! I must say that was delicious!

    Hostess: Yes. It took me hours, too!

18. *Old mother:*   Promise me — promise me you won't put me in one of those old people's homes, will

		you? You wouldn't abandon me like that, would you?
	Son:	No, of course not. We'll look after you ourselves, Mum. Don't worry.
19.	Radio interviewer:	Now, something which I'm sure will interest a lot of listeners, you actually knew Leonard Frinton personally, didn't you?
	Guest:	Yes, indeed. Leonard was an *extremely* dear friend. We were always very, *very* close — we were almost like brothers. It came as a terrible shock to me when he died. Of all the actors I have known, he was . . . how can I say it? . . . the most exquisitely talented . . .
20.	Customer:	Excuse me, I think I left my change on the counter. You didn't happen to see it by any chance, did you?
	Barman:	Nope. Sorry.

SECTION B

Activities requiring accurate communication of information between students

6. MYSTERY OBJECTS

Level Intermediate upwards

Outline
Each student has a small object hidden in his booth; its identity is known only to him or her. He or she records a precise description of it on his or her tape. All the students then move from booth to booth and try to identify their classmates' objects from their descriptions.

Preparation
!! (1) Put a number of different small objects (one for each student and a few over if possible) into a large bag. Try to include some *similar* objects (a couple of different cuff-links, two or three different lighters, or some different keys for example).

! (2) Pre-teach vocabulary of *size, shape, texture* and different *materials*. A list of these can be found on the next page.

! (3) Before the students go to the lab, erase about five minutes of tape in their booths (see page xiiì PRACTICAL NOTES at the beginning of the book).

Procedure
(1) When everyone is seated in the lab, go round with the bag of objects and let each student dip into it (without looking) and fish out an object without showing it to the others.

(2) Ask each to record a precise description of his or her object on the blank tape. Stress that no description should contain any mention of the name, purpose or colour of the object, nor must anything written on the object be quoted, otherwise the next stage of the activity will be far too easy. The description is thus limited to the size, shape, texture and composition of the object.

(3) When everyone has finished, go round again with the bag and discreetly take in each object.

(4) Now ask everyone to go from booth to booth and try to identify their classmates' objects from their descriptions of them. Encourage the more artistic ones to attempt drawings; the others can make out lists with the number of the booth and the object described in it.

(5) Stop them when you feel they have done enough: don't insist on them visiting every booth unless the class is quite small.

(6) Take the students back to the classroom (or to a place where there is a reasonably large table).

(7) Now empty the bag of objects out onto a table and let the students gather round to see if they recognise anything. If you can actually get your class sitting round the table, let them sort the objects out and place them in front of the people who described them. No-one must touch his or her own object of course.

(8) Ask the students if any of them had any trouble describing certain features of their objects and invite help and suggestions from the rest of the class.

Reproduction

Do the same exercise with numbered photos cut from magazines. You may need to pre-teach vocabulary pertaining to facial features. When each student has finished, collect up the photos and stick them to the walls of the lab with Blu-Tack.

Some useful vocabulary for **Mystery Objects**

		long
		wide
	inches	thick
It's about five	centimetres	high
	millimetres	tall
		in diameter
		across

It's about the same size as a . . . .

Shape

round	long	pointed
circular	short	L-shaped
spherical	wide	T-shaped
curved	broad	egg-shaped
square	thick	barrel-shaped
cubical	narrow	. . . . . . in cross-section
triangular	thin	tapering
hexagonal	cylindrical	(- off to a point)
conical	tubular	solid
oval	flat	hollow
elliptical	sharp	

Texture rough; coarse; jagged; milled; smooth; shiny; polished.

Materials

metal	wood	paint
iron	leather	glass
steel	ceramic	rubber
aluminium	china	plastic
copper	porcelain	nylon
brass	cloth	PVC
gold	material	perspex
silver	fabric	polythene
bronze	cardboard	
chrome	paper	

Miscellaneous

top	corner	underneath
bottom	surface	on (the) top of
side	underside	around
edge	inside	covering
rim	outside	enclosing
attached	a screw	a projection
screwed	a hole	a slit
fixed	a knob	a recess
glued	a ring	
welded	an indentation	
riveted	a rivet	

7. MAKE IT OR DRAW IT

Level   Intermediate upwards

Outline
The students record instructions in their booths for making a simple 'Lego' model or for drawing a simple cartoon. They then swap booths with each other and follow these instructions. Finally, they compare their results with the originals.

Preparation
!! (1)   Get hold of a box of 'Lego' or a similar children's building kit. If possible, try to get those little boxes containing a small 'Lego' model with an accompanying building diagram.

!! (2)   If you are only able to obtain the ordinary kind of Lego Kit, use it to make enough 'Lego' models for about half the class. The models should be different and very simple: not more than about ten bricks each. Your 'Lego' kit probably provides diagrams of such models.

!! (3)   Put the models in a bag and bring them to the next lab session.

!! (4)   Cut some cartoon jokes from a magazine or newspaper: choose those with strong visual humour or, better still, the captionless ones. Make sure there are enough for the other half of the class.

!! (5)   Pre-teach or revise *prepositions*.

 ! (6)   Erase about ten minutes of tape in the students' booths. (See PRACTICAL NOTES on page xiii).

Procedure
(1)   When everyone is sitting in the lab, give half of them a model each and the other half a cartoon each.

(2)   Ask them to record a precise description of how to make their model, or draw their cartoon, on their blank tape.

(3)   When they have finished, tell the 'Lego' people to dismantle their models and leave the pieces in their booths.

(4)   Tell the cartoonists to fold up their cartoons and put them in their pockets.

(5)   Go round the lab to make sure (3) and (4) have been done properly!

(6)   Now ask the 'Lego' people to swap booths with the cartoonists. Everyone now follows the instructions recorded in his new booth to make a 'Lego' model or to draw a cartoon.

(7)   If time and enthusiasm permit, let them move on to other booths. Don't forget that all 'Lego' models must be dismantled and all 'student' cartoons pocketed before booth occupants move on.

(8)   Finally, put all the cartoons and their originals on a big table along with the 'Lego' diagrams (if available).

(9)   Let the class discuss the results with each other.

Variation

The same style of activity could be tried with:

(a)   Some simple manipulations with Rubik's Cube. Cube-enthusiasts could record instructions for someone else to solve the cube three or four moves away from the solution.

(b)   Origami (making models by folding paper).

8. MY LIVING-ROOM

Level   Intermediate upwards

Outline

The students each draw a plan of their living room and then record a detailed description of it in their booths, explaining the position of the furniture and other things in it. They then swap booths with each other and each try to draw a plan of a partner's living room, following his recorded description.

Preparation

! (1)   Pre-teach prepositions and prepositional phrases:

next to	in the middle of
opposite	to the left of
between	halfway between
behind	in line with
in front of	as far as
around	parallel with
along	at right angles to

                etc., etc.

    Also pre-teach living-room vocabulary (see overleaf).

! (2)   Erase about ten minutes of tape in the students' booths. (See PRACTICAL NOTES on page xiii).

   (3)   This activity works best in pairs. If you have an odd number of students, you could join in the activity yourself.

Procedure

   (1)   Sit the students in the lab and ask each to draw a plan of his living room, labelling the different things in it.

   (2)   Now ask them each to record a precise description of how to draw their plan, on the blank tape.

   (3)   When they have done this, ask them to fold up their plans and put them away somewhere.

   (4)   Now ask each to choose a partner, swap booths with him or her, and follow the recorded instructions to draw a plan of the partner's living room.

   (5)   When they have finished, ask them to join up with their partners and comment on each other's plans.

Vocabulary

Furniture

coffee table
dining table
chair
armchair
sofa/settee/couch
cupboard
chest of drawers
sideboard
dresser
bureau
writing table
desk
cabinet
shelf/shelves
bookshelf
book-case

Permanent features

wall
window
bay window
French window
door
double doors
sliding doors
alcove
niche
ledge
window ledge/window sill
passage
steps
stairs
fireplace
mantelpiece

Electrical things

lamp
standard lamp
radio
television
telephone
hi-fi system/stereo system
loudspeakers

Fittings

curtain
carpet
rug
mat
radiator
heater

9. WANTED!

Level   Lower-intermediate upwards

Outline
Each student records a physical description of one of his colleagues in his booth. Everyone then moves from booth to booth trying to identify the person described in each.

Preparation
! (1)   Make sure your students know each other's names.
! (2)   Pre-teach vocabulary pertaining to physical appearance (facial features, build, complexion, etc.). Describe one or two of your students to the class to exemplify this, or bring in some magazine photos. (See page 35).
! (3)   Cut enough small slips of paper for everyone.
! (4)   Erase about five minutes of tape in the students' booths. (See PRACTICAL NOTES on page xiii).

Procedure
(1)   Sit the students in a circle and tell them to scrutinise the face of each of their classmates. Ask them to think (silently) about which of the words you pre-taught could apply to each.
(2)   Now sit them in the lab and give each a slip of paper. Ask them to write their names on them and then to fold them up.
(3)   Collect up the papers and re-distribute them at random.
(4)   Now explain that the person written on each paper is wanted by the police for armed robbery and can only be caught if a member of the public supplies a good description.
(5)   Tell them to record such a description on the blank portions of tape in their booths.
(6)   When everyone has finished, tell them to go from booth to booth and, listening to each description, to make a list of each booth number and the person described in it. Encourage the more artistic ones to draw sketches.
(7)   During this time, you could listen in and note any mistakes for correction later on.
(8)   Let the listening phase go on until you feel they have done enough. Don't insist on complete lists.

(9) Take the class to a place where there is a board. Divide the board up into numbered squares corresponding to the booths which were used in the lab.

(10) Now bring everyone up to the board and ask them to copy their lists onto it. If a square contains several identical names, then the corresponding description was easily recognisable. Any square containing different names corresponds to a hazier description.

(11) If any of your students did sketches, fix them to the corresponding square with some Blu-Tack.

(12) Ask any students whose names are in the same square to sit together.

(13) Now ask the others in the class if they think these people could really be mistaken for each other, and then ask why or why not.

Vocabulary

Shape of face
thin, bony, flat, round, plump, chubby, average, high cheekbones.

Hair
Form: straight, wavy, curly, frizzy, lank, greasy, wispy, rats' tails, tousled, messy, neat, untidy, back-length, shoulder-length, covering the ears, long, short, crew-cut, receding hairline, balding, bald patch, bald, fringe, lock, tuft, parting.

Colour: jet-black, black, dark, dark brown, auburn, light brown, mousy, ginger, red, honey-blond, blond(e), platinum-blonde, peroxide-blonde, greying, grey, silvery, white, blue-rinse, dull, shiny.

Complexion
pale, sallow, waxy, yellowish, brownish, darkish, black, reddish, ruddy, healthy, olive, olive-brown, pinkish, rosy, fresh.

Eyes
beady, round, slanting, piercing, sad, bright, sparkling, wide, narrow, staring, close-together, deep-set, bulging, olive, hooded, sleepy, bloodshot, cross-eyed.

Noses
aquiline, straight, snub, turned-up, hook, Roman, broken, flat, crooked, prominent, sharp, round, bulbous, distinguished, dainty.

Mouths and lips
small, wide, pursed, protruding, prominent, rosebud.

Chins

double, receding, prominent, cleft, dimpled, jutting, square, pointed, determined.

Other features

freckles, blemishes, moles, birthmarks, warts, spots, scars, wrinkles, lines, furrows, dimples, moustache, Mexican moustache, toothbrush moustache, soup-strainer, bushy, beard, goatee beard, well-groomed, well-trimmed, sideboards (sideburns) mutton-chops.

10. YOU CAN'T MISS IT!

Level   Lower-intermediate upwards

Outline

The students record instructions to direct someone to a certain destination on a map. They then swap booths and follow each other's directions.

N.B. This activity is based on directions given in *Britain:* roundabouts are to be taken *clockwise.*

Preparation

! (1)   Pre-teach expressions for giving directions.
! (2)   Erase about ten minutes of tape in the students' booths (See PRACTICAL NOTES on page xiii).
!! (3)   Make sure each student has a copy of the map (page 39).

Procedure

(1)   Sit the students in the lab and ask them to choose one of the numbered destinations on the map.
(2)   Now ask them to record, on the blank portion of tape, instructions to direct someone from 'start' to this destination, without mentioning the number.
(3)   When they have finished, ask them to swap booths and follow a colleague's directions to find the destination he chose.
(4)   Let the students move on to other booths if they want to.

Variation 1:   Lab rally   Lower-intermediate upwards

Outline

The students follow pre-recorded directions and all race to find the same destination.

Preparation

(1)   Pre-record 'Lab rally' (on the cassette) onto the students' booths.
(2)   Make sure everyone has a copy of the map.

Procedure

(1)   Tell your students to follow the pre-recorded directions as quickly as possible and to give you the destination written on a piece of paper when they have found it.

(2)   If you have a board in your lab, write up the names of the students in winning order (the first three should be enough).

(3)   Finally, explain the directions again for the benefit of anyone who got lost, using the tapescript on page 40).

Variation 2:   Sketch-map   Intermediate upwards

Outline

The students follow pre-recorded directions and draw a sketch-map.

Preparation

(1)   Make sure each student has a piece of paper and a pen.

Procedure

(1)   Record 'Sketch-map' (on the cassette) onto the students' tapes. (They can be in their booths listening).

(2)   Tell them that this corresponds to a friend giving directions to get to her new house, and that they must draw a sketch-map.

(3)   Let them listen at their own pace.

(4)   When they have finished, ask each to compare his or her result with a neighbour's (One possible interpretation of the directions is sketched below).

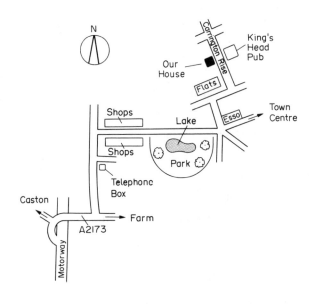

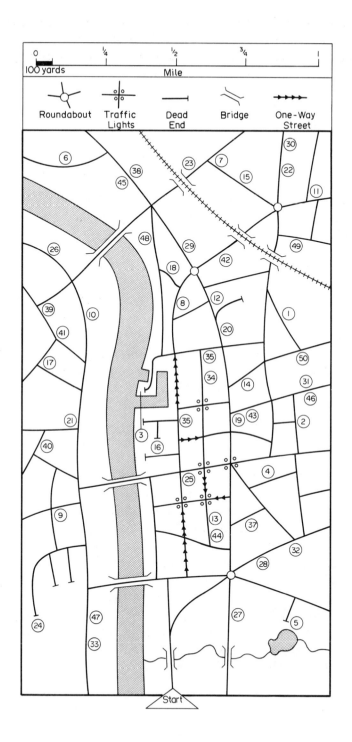

Tapescript for 'Lab rally'

Go straight on over the little bridge. When you get to the fork, bear right and carry on up to the roundabout. Take the third exit and then go on for about a quarter of a mile. You'll see a turning off on the left. Don't take this one, take the one after it, okay? When you get to the end of that road, there's a kind of staggered junction — you'll have to turn right and then left straight away. After that, take the first on the right — no, sorry — the first on the left, then turn right. Keep straight on and turn left just before you get to the bridge. Turn right at the T-junction and carry straight on over the roundabout. After that turn left — sharp left. At the end of the road turn left again and then turn right as soon as possible. Turn right again at the second set of traffic lights, carry straight on and turn left just after the bridge. Then take the first turning on the left, first on the right and it's about a third of a mile down the road — you can't miss it.

Tapescript for 'Sketch-map'

I think the best thing to do would be to draw a map, because it's a bit complicated. Have you got your pen and paper ready? Make sure it's a big piece. Oh, and you'd better start your map down on the bottom left-hand side because it sort of goes up to the right. Ready? So, you're coming up on the north-bound motorway. You come off the motorway on the A2173. The road goes up and then crosses over the motorway so you'll be going more or less east. Make sure you do cross over the motorway because if you take the fork that goes off to the left, you'll finish up in Caston. Anyway, after about two or three hundred yards, the road bends round to the left. Make sure you bear left because there's another little road that leads straight on to a farm or something, so you don't want that. After that — let's see . . . ah, yes, that's it — about a quarter of a mile after the bend you'll see a telephone box on the corner. Don't turn there but take the next one up on the right. You'll go past some shops and after that there's a kind of park with a lake on the right. A bit further along, you come to a kind of crossroads with five roads. When you get here, you have to turn sharp left. There's an Esso garage on the corner, on the right as you go past. Make sure you turn sharp left otherwise you'll end up in the town centre and the traffic's pretty awful on Saturdays. You'll see a big block of flats right in front of you at the end of the street. Turn right, then left into Carrington Rise and our house is about halfway up on the left. Actually, it's just next to the block of flats. There's no number on the door but you can't miss it — we're just opposite the King's Head. Okay? You don't want me to go over it again, do you? See you tonight then about eight. Bye.

Vocabulary

				the roundabout
				the fork
Keep			reach	the T-junction
				the staggered junction
Go	straight on	till you	get to	the 1st/2nd set of traffic lights
Carry		as far as		the end of the road
				the crossroads
		up to		the intersection

Turn left/right at the traffic lights
Take the second turning on the left and the first on the right
Turn right, then right again
Turn right, then left
Take the left fork
Bear left
Follow the road round to the left.
Turn right just before/after you get to the bridge
Turn sharp left
At the roundabout, take the second exit
Carry straight on over the roundabout
a one-way street
a cul-de-sac
a dead end

	on your left as you go past
	on the corner
The supermarket's	halfway up/down the street
	just opposite the post office
	on the left-hand side

(2) COUPLE FORCED TO SELL DREAM HOME

A couple who spent 15 years turning an old cottage into a dream home have been forced to resell it at its original price.

Peter Skipton, a 41-year old plumber, and his wife Margaret, of Hillcroft, Bedfordshire, bought the cottage from Christopher Hawker, an insurance broker, for £2,500 in 1965.

But the Skiptons failed to notice a clause in the contract stating that Mr. Hawker could buy back the cottage at any time for the original price.

A heartbroken Mr. Skipton said: "We have wasted 15 years of our life turning that pile of bricks into a decent home. I am disgusted that a man I trusted as a gentleman could act so deceitfully."

Mr. Hawker offered the couple an extra £2,000 to compensate for the work carried out on the 18th century cottage, but the Skiptons refused to accept the sale conditions and the case was taken to court.

Mr. Hawker's right to repurchase the property was upheld by the High Court, and the Skiptons now have less than a week to remove their belongings from the cottage.

(3) PINK WEDDING

A French couple solved the problem of an expensive wedding suit and wedding dress — they got married in the nude.

Pierre and Christelle Champfort were married yesterday on a sun-soaked naturist beach near Perpignan in the South of France.

Everyone present — including the priest who married the Adam and Eve couple — was wearing nothing more than a smile.

Said Pierre: "We were rather revolted with the idea of wasting so much money on expensive clothes that would never be worn again. Christelle and I are naturists, like many of our friends, so we decided to have a wedding with a difference."

His attractive, dark-haired bride added: "We sent invitations to all our friends and family, and we were surprised to see how many came, even though most of them had never been on a naturist beach before."

French readers will be disappointed to learn that their wedding photo will *not* be appearing in any French newspapers.

(4) SERIOUS WEST COUNTRY FLOODING

More than 50 families have been forced to abandon their homes after serious flooding in the Wye valley.

The river Wye, which flows through an area of flat country close to the towns of Ferron and Coltring, burst its banks yesterday after a fall of more than 10 inches of rain in five days.

The families, some of whose homes are under three feet of water, are being lodged by friends or neighbours, or in emergency centres set up in the local schools and church halls.

People living in the area are also threatened with the possibility of gas explosions and a polluted water supply.

Athough no-one has been reported injured, several sheep have been drowned, and the cost of damage to property including crops, buildings and vehicles, has been estimated at well over a million pounds.

(5) COUPLE ELOPE USING CB

Irene, 16, and her 17-year old boyfriend Clive, both from Glasgow, ran away from home after planning their escape by CB radio.

Mr. and Mrs. Pringle, the girl's parents, set off on a 400-mile journey yesterday after police had traced the couple's whereabouts to Southend.

Mr. Pringle had forbidden the couple's romance, but Clive bought two CB radios, giving one to Irene, so that they could still keep in touch every night.

Then, a month ago, Irene left her home by climbing down a ladder which Clive had put up to her window.

They have both kept in touch with their parents to assure them that they are all right, although they refuse to reveal where they are.

Mr. Pringle, a 42-year old electrician, said that if his daughter agreed to come back, he would no longer forbid her to see Clive.

(6) BOEING 727 HI-JACKED

A Boeing 727 leaving Helsinki for London was hi-jacked late yesterday afternoon by two armed men.

Shortly after the plane took off with 157 passengers and crew, the two men forced their way into the cockpit, threatened the pilot with pistols, and ordered him to fly the jet to Rotterdam.

Dutch security police were already surrounding the airport by the time the plane landed at 6.45 yesterday evening.

One of the hi-jackers later made contact with the airport authorities using the plane's radio, demanding the release of certain men from Rotterdam's high-security prison.

The prisoners in question are serving long sentences for terrorism offences, including the bombing of a Dutch hotel in 1977 which killed seven people.

The hi-jackers have threatened to begin executing their hostages one by one every hour unless their demands are satisfied by midday tomorrow.

(7) 'BIONIC' HAND FOR ACCIDENT VICTIM

A man who was severely injured in a dockside accident two years ago, is to be given the first 'bionic' hand.

Roger Coates, a 37-year old foreman from Caston, near Portsmouth, was working under a transport container which fell, severely crushing his right hand and forearm, when one of the supporting chains broke.

Surgeons fought to save the mutilated hand, but eventually had to amputate it.

The new mechanical hand will be permanently attached to Mr. Coates' forearm and powered by a small unit strapped to his waist.

When asked what he hoped to be able to do with his new hand, he joked: "I wont be able to play Flamenco guitar, but all the things you take for granted, like getting dressed, eating and driving, will be a lot easier".

The operation will be performed at St. Margaret's hospital in July, and is expected to cost in the region of £560,000

12. SELF-DICTATION

Level Beginners upwards

Outline

You dictate a short passage to the class. The class repeats what you say after the pauses and their repetition is recorded onto their tapes. At the end of the passage, the students listen to their recording and make a transcript of it. The 'dictation' is thereby provided only by the students' own voices.

Preparation

!! (1) The students must be able to rewind and listen to their repetition of your dictation without *your* voice being audible on their tapes.
There are two ways you could achieve this; choose the one which works best for your lab:
   (a) If the booths have separate 'teacher' and 'student' tracks ask the students to turn the 'teacher' volume down to zero during the replay. Check beforehand to make sure this is effective.
   (b) Stop their machines while you are dictating and start them for each repetition. Make sure these manipulations are not too cumbersome and that the stop-start noises won't annoy the students!

!! (2) Choose a suitable passage for dictation and decide where the pauses are to be.

!! (3) Make a copy of the passage for each student.

Procedure

   (1) Sit the students in the lab. Explain to them that they are to repeat what you say as accurately as possible. (You might prefer to tell them *why* later on).

   (2) Dictate the passage according to the method you chose in part (1) of the 'Preparation'. You might find it helpful to cue the repetitions by waving your hand, or some other gesture.

   (3) Ask them to rewind, listen again at their own pace and write out the passage using the recording of their own voice.

   (4) When they have finished this, give them each a copy of the passage and ask them to match it with their own, ringing the mistakes in their own work.

   (5) Collect up their work. By having a look through the pile of 'ringed' dictations, you may get a good idea of what kind of words are more frequently misunderstood (contractions, weak forms, etc.).

Variation

The same as the preceding activity but ask the students to swap booths just before the writing phase (part (3) of **Preparation**). Each now has to rely on a classmate's voice-recording to supply the dictation.

13. TELEPHONE SITUATIONS

Level   Intermediate upwards

Outline

Two students in different booths are given a role to play. They are then put into intercommunication with each other and act out a telephone conversation with each other. The others listen and are later invited to supply any corrections at the end of the conversation. There are other situations for other pairs to act out. The lab provides a fairly realistic simulation of a real telephone situation since there is no eye contact, and voices are relayed via headphones.

Preparation

!! (1)   Before attempting this activity, make sure that:

EITHER

   (a)   two students in different booths can communicate with each other via their microphones, and be heard by the others in their booths

OR

   (b)   a student sitting at the teacher's console and a student sitting in one of the booths can communicate with each other via their microphones, and be heard by the others in their booths.

!! (2)   If possible, experiment with a couple of colleagues or students beforehand to check this arrangement.

! (3)   Pre-record about five minutes of music in the students' booths.

! (4)   Pre-teach some simple telephone language:

"Hello, is that X? This is Y speaking".

"I'm ringing about . . . "

"Sorry, could you say that again, please?"

"The line's very bad, could you speak a little louder, please?"

! (5)   Look at the roles on pages 50–52 and decide which students are going to assign them to.

Procedure

(1)   Sit the students in the lab.

(2)   Ask student B in the first pair to listen to the music. (He must not hear what you are going to say to A.)

(3)   Now read A's role to student A and the rest of the class.

(4)   Now ask student A to listen to his music while you explain B's role to B and the rest of the class.

(5) Put A into intercommunication with B (as in step 1 of **Preparation**). Say: RING! RING!'' to signal the start of the conversation.

(6) During the conversation, jot down the mistakes made by the two participants.

(7) Make sure the conversation doesn't go on too long: four or five minutes should be enough, especially if you want to let the others have a turn.

(8) When the conversation has finished, invite corrections to the mistakes you noted from the rest of the class.

(9) Tell the class to bear in mind the corrections to these mistakes in their own situations later on.

(10) Repeat the preceding steps with another pair.

Paired 'conflict' roles for telephone situations

Situation 1: Tough meat.

Student A

Last Friday, you bought a piece of meat for a special Sunday lunch with some friends. Unfortunately, the meat was extremely tough, and ruined the whole meal. You are very angry, especially as this is not the first time your butcher, Mr/s Rump, has given you tough meat. Phone to complain, and demand satisfaction!

Student B

You are Mr/s. Rump, a high-class family butcher. One of your customers phones to complain about some meat. S/he is one of those obnoxious people who enjoy complaining about everything. As you know how demanding s/he is, you always give him/her the very best meat. Be polite, but don't give in to his/her demands!

Situation 2: No Breakfast.

Student A

You are Mr/s Richards. You are staying in a very posh hotel. Last night, before you went to bed, you told reception to send your breakfast up to your room (No. 806) for seven o'clock. It's now half past eight and you are very hungry and very angry. Phone reception to find out what the devil they have done with it!

Student B

You are the receptionist at an expensive hotel with an excellent reputation. A guest phones down to say that s/he didn't get breakfast in his/her room (No. 806) as ordered. You know that s/he is mistaken as you took it up personally to that room at exactly seven o'clock.

Situation 3: Last evening together.

Student A (male)

Tomorrow, you leave to do your military service a thousand miles away. This is your last chance to spend an evening with Anna. Phone her to invite her out somewhere. Try to charm her a little as she is very shy and difficult to persuade.

Student B (female)

A man you know phones you to invite you out with him. Be as polite as you can but don't let him persuade you. He's very boring and ugly and he's got bad breath. You must find a good excuse!

Situation 4: A day off.

Student A

Next weekend, your best friend is getting married in New York. You would very much like to go but this means leaving on Friday morning. You feel that you deserve a day off as you work a lot of overtime, sometimes work during the lunch hour and often take important work home to finish. Phone your boss, Mr/s Grumble, to explain.

Student B

You are Mr/s Grumble, the boss of a big firm. An employee phones you to ask for a day off. This particular person is getting on your nerves as s/he is never on time, comes back from the pub half-drunk at three o'clock in the afternoon, and is always asking for time off for various fictitious reasons. This time you've had enough!

Situation 5: The bomb

Student A

You were digging in your garden a few moments ago when you suddenly uncovered an enormous, unexploded wartime bomb. When you touched it, it started ticking! If it explodes, it'll demolish the whole house! Phone the police and get help . . . quickly!

Student B

You are the sergeant on duty at the local police station. The station has recently been inconvenienced by a series of hoaxes involving unexploded bombs. The person responsible is believed to be a lunatic who always gives a false address. Next time you get a bomb call, you keep the person talking as long as possible so that your colleagues can trace the call and catch this imbecile.

51

Situation 6: The compromising photo

Student A

You are very famous and influential politician. Just as you were leaving your hotel this morning, there was a big bank robbery next door. A journalist who happened to be there took a sensational photo. You are sure that *you* are on it too. The problem is, you were with your mistress/boyfriend. Your wife/husband thinks you are in Paris for a meeting. If the photo is published, you will be ruined. Phone the journalist, Jo Scoop, to bribe him/her not to. Don't give your name as s/he is always looking for sensational stories!

Student B

You are Jo Scoop, a journalist. This morning you took a sensational photo of criminals fleeing after a big bank robbery. Someone phones you and ask you not to publish the picture, which is worth at least £100,000. Very suspicious! There could be another big story for you here! Find out as much as you can!

14. EAVESDROPPING

Level   Upper-intermediate to advanced

Outline

A story is composed of nine dialogues. The dialogues are all linked with a mysterious object. The students can only guess the identity and purpose of the object by listening to the dialogues and then communicating their findings, since they are divided into three different listening groups and do not hear the same dialogues.

This activity might be a good lead-in to a subsequent discussion on advertising or the mass-media.

Preparation

(1)   Divide the booths arbitrarily into three groups, A, B and C. The groups should be as nearly equal as possible but it doesn't matter if they aren't exactly equal.

(2)   Before the students come to the lab,

record dialogues A1, A2 and A3 onto group A's tapes

dialogues B1, B2 and B3 onto group B's tapes

and dialogues C1, C2 and C3 onto group C's tapes

Note: If your lab doesn't cater for this kind of selective recording, record all the dialogues onto everyone's tapes, then rewind. Wind group B's tapes forward again as far as the beginning of the B dialogues, and group C's tapes as far as the C dialogues. (See also on page xiii).

Procedure

(1)   Sit the students in the lab. (If you recorded *all* the dialogues onto their tapes (see 'Note' above), make sure they don't alter the position of their tapes when they sit down.

(2)   Ask each group to listen to the first dialogue on their tapes. (Group A hears dialogue A1, group B hears B1 and group C hears C1).

(3)   Encourage them to ask you, *language* questions during the listening phase, but don't elucidate any of the ambiguities in the dialogues. Note-taking can be encouraged.

(4)   When they have had enough time to grasp the essential ideas in the dialogues, ask them to move into groups of three containing one person from each listening group. Any remaining people can join any group.

(5) Ask them to share and discuss their findings; each person has information which the others need to elucidate the mystery.

(6) Move round the groups to see how they are getting on. Encourage exchange of personnel between groups, especially those containing weaker students.

(7) When you feel the discussion has gone on long enough, ask them to return to their original booths.

(8) Now ask each of them to listen to the next dialogue on their tapes (A2, B2 or C2), which represents a further development in the story. Those students who have time may also rewind to listen to their first dialogue again if they want to.

(9) Ask them to form small discussion groups as before. They need not contain the same people as the first time.

(10) Now bring them back to their booths to listen to their final dialogue (and either of the two previous ones if need be).

(11) Ask them to form small discussion groups as before.

(12) They should, by now, have a good idea about the object and its function. If this is not the case, take them to a place where they can discuss as a whole class, with your guidance.

Key to the story

Jeremy Addison, an electronics engineer, has perfected a device which can be used to influence people's decisions. The device is contained in a small, portable box. When it is switched on, it emits an inaudible high-frequency sound (ultrasound). The sound is tuned to influence two parts of the 'target' person's brain. Firstly, it stimulates the 'pleasure centre', so that the 'target' person associates whatever is said to him at that moment with a sensation of pleasure. Secondly, it reduces the effect of the 'inhibition centre', the part of the brain which inhibits irresponsible decisions or behaviour.

The device can be used person to person, or be attached to a telephone to influence the person being called. It can be used in radio and television broadcasts to favour the effects of advertisements — or even party political broadcasts. The potential is clearly devastating.

Key to the dialogues

A1:   Addison's friend, Chris, uses the device to pick up a girl at a party.

B1:   In the pub, Chris boasts of his conquest using the device. Addison announces that he has found a suitable manufacturer for it.

C1:   Finch, the director of Finch Electronics, has come to see Addison about his invention. At the end, he realises that Addison had actually used the device on him to persuade him to come.

A2: Finch tells Bartlett, his production manager, to stop production of their new burglar alarm so that the device can be produced instead.

B2: Second meeting between Finch and Addison. Finch wants more convincing evidence that the device actually works. Addison suggests that he should use it to phone up one of his difficult customers.

C2: Addison explains to Bartlett, by way of a symbolic story, how the device works.

A3: The Commissioner and an inspector from the Police Special Branch discuss the far-reaching implications of the device and the urgent need to capture the people involved with it.

B3: The inspector has consulted a university professor to explain to him how the device works.

C3: Finch phones up one of his difficult customers, Sapworth, who recently turned down an order with Finch for a burglar alarm system. Sapworth agrees to a second meeting to re-discuss. Finch realises that he would never have accepted to do this normally. He is convinced that the device, which was switched on during the conversation, influenced Sapworth.

Tapescript

Eavesdropping

Dialogue A1

Chris:	Hello, Wendy! I didn't know y– Oh, sorry. I thought you were someone I knew. 'Scuse me.
Charlotte:	That's all right. My name's Charlotte, actually.
Chris:	I'm Chris — a friend of Pete's. You know, you look just like another girl I know.
Charlotte:	Well, I hope you're not *too* disappointed.
Chris:	Oh, no! Actually, the other girl isn't as — er — nice-looking as you.
Charlotte:	I see. So you're Chris, are you?
Chris:	Mmm. It's funny, I've been here for hours, but I don't remember seeing you before.
Charlotte:	Well, I didn't come till after ten. Anyway, I'll have to be going soon. It's nearly two.
Chris:	Mmm. A lot of people have already gone. It was a great party, though. How are you getting back?
Charlotte:	Well, with Sylvie over there, I suppose.
Chris:	*I* could take you back, if you like. My car's just out the front.

55

Charlotte:	Well, that's very kind of you, but I've arranged to go back with Sylvie.
Chris:	Why don't you come back with me? You could stop by for some coffee, if you like.
Charlotte:	Well . . . okay . . . why not? If you're sure it's no trouble.
Pete:	Did you see that?
Jim:	What?
Pete:	Chris!
Jim:	What about him?
Pete:	He's just left — with Charlotte!
Jim:	Charlotte? What, Sylvie's blonde friend? But she doesn't even know him!
Pete:	Well, she seems to know him well enough *now*.
Jim:	Lucky devil. How does he do it?
Pete:	I don't know. Must be his natural, irresistible, magnetic charm.
Jim:	Huh. What was that thing he was carrying about?
Pete:	I don't know. One of those new calculators, I suppose.

Tapescript

Eavesdropping

Dialogue B1

Barmaid:	That's two pounds forty-five, please. Thanks very much.
Chris:	Thanks. There you go.
Addison:	Thanks, Chris. Cheers.
Chris:	Cheers. Hey! Your little box of tricks is bloody fantastic!
Addison:	Shh! Keep it down! Not so loud!
Chris:	Ah, don't worry. Who'd know what we were talking about anyway?
Addison:	You never know. Anyway, what have you been doing with it?
Chris:	I took it to Pete's party last night. I wish you could've been there. You'd've been proud!
Addison:	All right, I can guess what you used it for. Or should I say, *who* you used it *on*. Anyway, I want it back. I need it tomorrow afternoon.
Chris:	What do *you* want it for?
Addison:	Someone's coming round tomorrow.
Chris:	Who did you manage to get?

Addison:	The director of Finch Electronics, would you believe!
Chris:	Finch Electronics! You got *Finch*!
Addison:	Shh! Not so loud! I keep telling you, you never know who's listening.
Chris:	Finch, eh? That's really marvellous.
Addison:	Well, Finch Electronics *was* the perfect choice. After all, you know what kind of stuff they manufacture.
Chris:	Ah, no. There's no doubt there. Jeremy. They're the best people for the job.

Tapescript

Eavesdropping

Dialogue C1

Finch:	Is this it, then?
Addison:	Yep, that's it.
Finch:	Doesn't look much.
Addison:	You could say that was the whole idea.
Finch:	Yes, I see what you mean.
Addison:	Well, there it is. Three years of hard work — sleepless nights — a nagging wife . . . I hope, after all this, you're interested, Mr. Finch.
Finch:	Does it work?
Addison:	Ha ha!
Finch:	What's so funny?
Addison:	Does it work!
Finch:	Well, does it? I suppose you've tried it.
Addison:	I'm sorry, Mr. Finch, I'm being a bit rude. Yes, I have tried it — several times.
Finch:	And?
Addison:	I'm pretty sure it works.
Finch:	How can you *be* so sure?
Addison:	Well, you *are* here, aren't you?
Finch:	What do you mean?
Addison:	*You* came to *me*, Mr. Finch. That's rather unusual, isn't it? I mean normally, a salesman goes to the buyer when he wants to sell something. *Not* vice-versa.
Finch:	I see. So, if I understand correctly, Mr. Addison, you've already tried your little gadget on *me*.
Addison:	I hope my little demonstration has impressed you, Mr. Finch.

Eavesdropping

Dialogue A2

Finch:	Shirley?
Shirley:	Yes, Mr. Finch?
Finch:	Ask Bartlett to come in now, please — oh, and I don't want to be disturbed for the next half-hour. We've got something rather important to discuss. If anyone phones, tell them to call back later.
Shirley:	Right, Mr. Finch.
Finch:	Come in.
Bartlett:	Mr. Finch.
Finch:	Have a seat. How are things?
Bartlett:	Fine, fine. Oh, those new components have arrived. We should be able to produce our new alarm very soon. There's just a little problem of interference to solve.
Finch:	Listen: I want you to forget about the alarm for the moment. You'll have to drop it.
Bartlett:	Drop it?
Finch:	Yes. Something else has come up.
Bartlett:	But we're only three weeks away from —
Finch:	I know that, Mr. Bartlett, but as I said, there's something else. Something *big*.
Bartlett:	It'd have to be *very* big to take precedence over the new alarm.
Finch:	Listen: this is so big that I don't think even *I* can grasp all the implications. Can I trust you, Mr. Bartlett?
Bartlett:	I sincerely hope so, sir. I don't think I've let you down in the past.
Finch:	Good. Because what I'm going to tell you must not leave these four walls. Is that door closed?

Eavesdropping

Dialogue B2

Finch:	From what Mr. Bartlett tells me, Mr. Addison, your little device seems to be based on very firm principles. I trust his *theoretical* evaluation, but —

Addison:	But you'd like more concrete proof.
Finch:	Exactly.
Addison:	I'm sure that can be arranged. Have you had any — er — difficult customers lately?
Finch:	Difficult?
Addison:	Yes. I mean, for example, potential buyers, potential customers who weren't interested, or weren't convinced.
Finch:	I could give you a list of failed missions *that* long. Fortunately, the list of successful missions is just as long.
Addison:	That still represents only fifty percent success. Tell me about one of the people on your list — your failure list.
Finch:	Sapworth. Sapworth almost signed a big contract with us for some ultrasonic movement detectors. They wanted to use them as security alarms in their warehouses.
Addison:	Weren't they satisfied with them?
Finch:	Well, they were impressed enough with our demonstrations. Those alarms are the best of their kind in the world. In a huge warehouse, nobody could move so much as a packet of detergent without the system registering it. It really is an excellent alarm device.
Addison:	So why weren't they interested.?
Finch:	Cost. Our stuff is very expensive. We were already offering it at the lowest possible price, but it was still too much for them.
Addison:	Could you find some pretext for phoning them up?
Finch:	Again?
Addison:	Yes. But this time we'll use a little more . . . persuasion.

Tapescript

Eavesdropping

Dialogue C2

Bartlett:	Mmm. A nice little piece of electronics. I don't recognise some of the parts in here.
Addison:	They're from Holland.
Bartlett:	Holland? How does the thing work?
Addison:	It should be quite easy to explain to someone with your qualifications, Mr. Bartlett.
Bartlett:	Okay, I'm listening.
Addison:	Are you married?

Bartlett:	No, why?
Addison:	Have you got a girlfriend?
Bartlett:	Listen, I don't really see what that's go to do —
Addison:	You will. Listen. Just imagine for a moment. It's hot, the sun's shining, the birds are singing, and there's a nice cool breeze rustling the leaves in the trees.
Bartlett:	Very romantic.
Addison:	You're sitting on a park bench. There's a really good-looking girl sitting on the other end. But between you and her, there's an old man. You'd like to start a conversation with the girl but you feel a bit embarrassed because of the old man. You're hoping he'll get up and go away. Eventually, he does. Now, you're alone with the girl on the park bench — with the sound of the birds and the breeze. You're quite a good looking chap. What do you think your chances are?
Bartlett:	I don't know. That could depend on a lot of things. Listen, are you going to tell me how this thing works, or are you going to tell me symbolic stories all afternoon?
Addison:	Let me finish. Let's imagine something a bit different. The same scene: you, the girl, and the old man in the middle. This time, it's a miserable, grey day. The old man doesn't get up and go away. He gets his paper out and starts reading it. What do you think your chances are now?
Bartlett:	Well, I suppose that in those circumstances, you wouldn't stand much chance at all.
Addison:	My little box, Mr. Bartlett, gets rid of the old man, makes you look like a film star, and gives instant sunshine. Have you understood my little story? It *is* rather symbolic, I must admit.

Tapescript

Eavesdropping

Dialogue A3

Inspector:	Do you realise, Commissioner, how horrific the implications are?
Commissioner:	I'm just beginning to imagine.
Inspector:	Just think of the impact on advertising, for example.

Commissioner:	Advertising is only the beginning. What worries me are the political applications. It's only a question of time before they make a much more powerful version. One which works not just on one person, but hundreds. A whole army could be manipulated.
Inspector:	With radio and television, a whole country.
Commissioner:	Are you sure it would work with radio and television?
Inspector:	Why not? It works with telephones.
Commissioner:	Not the old ones.
Inspector:	No. Apparently, only the new ones are capable of handling the very high frequencies.
Commissioner:	Listen, Inspector, if we're going to get all the people involved in this, we'll have to be very careful.
Inspector:	We already know who's involved.
Commissioner:	*Some* of the people involved. It's absolutely essential that *all* the people mixed up in this be caught — and caught fast. If we only arrest some, the others'll very quickly run off to another country, and exploit their infernal contraption there.
Inspector:	We've been watching Addison's movements lately.
Commissioner:	I want that man watched twenty-four hours a day every day. We must know who he's contacting. Your boys'll have to be very discreet, Inspector. If he suspects for one moment that twenty Special Branch coppers are breathing down his neck, everything'll be ruined. There'll be nothing we can do.

Tapescript

Eavesdropping

Dialogue B3

Professor:	Well, it's not very easy to explain, but I'll try. Do you know a little about biology, Inspector?
Inspector:	Not much, I'm afraid.
Professor:	To understand the box, you must first understand a little about the brain.
Inspector:	All I know, about the brain, Professor, is that it's grey and it thinks.
Professor:	Ha ha ha! Well, I'll try to explain it as simply as possible. In the brain, there is a certain region called the pleasure centre.

61

Inspector:	The pleasure centre.
Professor:	Yes. When you see a pretty girl, eat your favourite food or hear your favourite music, the pleasure centre in your brain is stimulated, and you have a sensation of pleasure. Do you understand? It it clear so far?
Inspector:	Yes, yes. I've followed you so far.
Professor:	In another part of the brain, there is another kind of centre. We could call it the — er — inhibition centre.
Inspector:	What does the inhibition centre do?
Professor:	Well, imagine that you're with a friend, and he offers you a big glass of whisky. In five minutes you have to drive home. Would you accept, and drink the whisky?
Inspector:	No, not if I had to drive afterwards.
Professor:	Of course not. Because the inhibition centre in your brain tells you not to. Like a kind of conscience or responsibility. The inhibition centre helps you to resist temptation, if you like. It stops you from doing irresponsible things.
Inspector:	I see. You explain things very well but what's the connection with the box?
Professor:	Well, it seems that this little box actually influences these two centres.
Inspector:	How can it do that?
Professor:	Ultrasound. Very high frequency sound. So high that you can't hear it. If you turn the box on and point it at someone, it stimulates his pleasure centre. Anything you say to him will be associated with a sensation of pleasure. At the same time, the box limits the inhibition centre, so the person has a tendency to do irresponsible things. Things he wouldn't normally do.

Tapescript

Eavesdropping

Dialogue C3

Receptionist:	Sapworth, good morning.
Finch:	Good morning. Could you put me through to Mr. Francis Sapworth, please?
Receptionist:	Certainly; who's calling, please?
Finch:	This is Finch from Finch Electronics.
Receptionist:	Hold the line please.

Sapworth:	Hello?
Finch:	Mr. Sapworth?
Sapworth:	Speaking.
Finch:	Finch here from Finch Electronics. Mr. Sapworth, I think we may be able to come to an agreement about the alarm order. If it were possible, I'd like to make an appointment with you to talk about it.
Sapworth:	I very much appreciate your attention, Mr. Finch, but, as I think I made clear during your last visit, the alarm systems you proposed really are far too expensive.
Finch:	Could be perhaps discuss it? I'm sure we could come to an agreement.
Sapworth:	I'm sorry, I'm a very busy man. I really can't afford to —
Finch:	I'm sure we could come to some agreement.
Sapworth:	Well . . . all right —
Finch:	This afternoon? Four thirty?
Sapworth:	Yes, all right. I've noted it. Four thirty.
Finch:	Thank you Mr. Sapworth. See you at four thirty. Unbelievable!
Addison:	Yes, isn't it? Oh, don't forget to take the box with you at four thirty. It works very nicely on the phone but even better at close range.

15. THREE-PART STORIES

Level   Lower-intermediate upwards

Outline
In the lab, the students are put into three listening groups. Each group hears a different part of a three-part story. After everyone has had the time to assimilate their part of the story, they leave their booths, form groups of three (one representative from each listening group), and share the different information they have in order to piece the story together. The students can only understand the whole story if they have understood each of the three parts properly.

Preparation
! (1)   Before the students come to the lab, divide the booths arbitrarily into three groups of equal (or nearly equal) number. Record a different part of the three part story onto each group's tapes (See page 0).

Procedure
(1)   Sit the students in the lab and let them listen at their own pace to their respective parts of the story. Let them ask you questions, or listen again, if they want to.
(2)   Now ask everyone to leave their booths and form groups of three; each trio must contain one person from each listening group. 'Odd' people can tack onto any trio.
(3)   Explain that, in order to understand the whole story, they must share the information they have with each other.
      Note: The 'trios' need not be adhered to: you could encourage some students to confer with people from their *own* listening group to check details. You could also encourage exchange *between* trios.

Development
Once the story has been more or less elucidated, you could ask your students to write their version of it.

Reproduction
Almost any short story can be adapted for this kind of activity, and be divided into two, three or even four parts. Make sure each part contains something

more or less essential to the story as a whole. An excellent source of adaptable stories are the three (graded) books:

Elementary/Intermediate/Advanced Stories for Reproduction (L. A. Hill, Oxford University Press)

Tapescript

The Dragon Hotel

It was November, and the Devonshire countryside was a miserable grey-green smear. The Dragon Hotel was warm and quiet. The only other people staying there, apart from me, were a couple of elderly ladies and a travelling salesman of about forty.

One Thursday evening, after dinner, I was sitting in my room reading. I glanced at the clock on the mantelpiece. A quarter to ten. Suddenly, in the big mirror, I noticed a young man standing in the doorway. He was wearing a white jacket and had a big blond moustache. I turned round quickly and said: "I'm sorry, did you knock? I didn't hear . . ." but he had already gone. I didn't remember seeing his face at the hotel before. He was obviously a new waiter who had mistaken my room for someone else's. As it was getting late, I put my book away and went to bed.

The following evening, I was just finishing the last chapter of my book when suddenly I caught sight of the same young man in the mirror again. "Don't forget your window, sir." he said politely. When I turned round, he had already gone. I looked at the window. It was open. The maid had forgotten to close it when she was airing the room this morning. I hadn't noticed because I was sitting right next to the fire.

On the Saturday morning, when I was getting dressed, I couldn't find my Saint Christopher chain in my drawer. As it was quite small, I thought that it had perhaps gone under the paper in the drawer. I lifted up the brown paper and found another layer of newspaper underneath. It was yellow and old, and I was curious to see what date it was. November the tenth 1957. Exactly twenty-five years ago! To the day! I noticed one of the headlines: 'MAN DIES IN HOTEL BLAZE'. I read the rest of the story and discovered to my complete astonishment that the hotel which had burnt in 1957 was the Dragon Hotel — the one I was staying in now!

I completely forgot about my Saint Christopher and went down to the breakfast room where I was served a good plate of steaming porridge and a pot of tea. The waitress was a pleasant-faced woman with blonde hair tied up in a bun. Her grey-green eyes seemed to reflect the sad colours of the winter countryside. I was fascinated by the old news item I had found, and I asked her about the fire. "It was an awful tragedy," she said. "The fire spread very quickly because the window was open in one of the rooms upstairs — or that's what they say." I could tell from her voice that she had been working at the Dragon Hotel at the time of the fire. I could also tell from her face that I had revived an unpleasant memory so I tactfully changed the subject and asked her for another pot of tea.

After breakfast, I went for a walk to the next town and spent a couple of hours looking round some antique shops. I wanted to find a little something to take back to my wife but I couldn't stop thinking about the Dragon Hotel and the intriguing coincidences of the newspaper. I had a strange feeling that perhaps they were more than just coincidences . . . perhaps, in some way, it was not just by chance that I had found that old newspaper.

I finally bought a pair of silver sugar tongs and went back to the hotel. I was just walking into reception when I noticed a brown wallet lying under the hatstand. There was nobody in reception at that time of day so I decided to look inside the wallet myself to see whose it might be. I couldn't see any name. I didn't want to be indiscreet but it seemed that the best way of finding the owner would be to look at the contents. In one of the pockets, I saw the edge of a photo. I pulled it out carefully. It was an old black-and-white picture which had been taken on the seafront. I immediately recognised the hotel waitress — her blonde hair and the shape of her eyes and mouth. In the photo, she was young, pretty and smiling. Standing next to her, his arm tenderly around her waist, was a young man. He had a big blond moustache.

SECTION C

Activities in which the student provides appropriate and spontaneous responses to a series of stimuli

16. LISTEN! WHAT'S GOING ON?

Level   Lower intermediate upwards

Outline

The students hear a series of sounds pre-recorded on their tapes. They then record a simultaneous commentary to accompany the sounds.

Preparation

! (1)   Listen to the sounds recorded on the cassette yourself.

! (2)   Pre-teach certain expressions of *speculation* and *deduction* if you feel your students will need them:

He *could be* frying an egg.

He *must be* hungry.

He *might be* late for work.

He *can't be* a very tidy person.

He *must have* been to a party last night.

He *can't have* gone to bed until the early hours.

It *sounds as* if he's trying to unlock the door.

It *sounds like* an alarm clock.

Perhaps he's drunk.

Don't, however, put any ideas about the sounds themselves into their heads: let them form their own.

Procedure

(1)   Record the sounds onto the students' tapes. (They can be in their booths listening).

(2)   Ask the students to listen again and, when they are ready, to record a running commentary onto their student tracks to accompany the sounds.

(3)   Listen in discreetly and note down any mistakes worthy of explanation later on.

(4)   When some of the students have finished, ask them to swap booths with each other to compare commentaries.

Development

(A)   Ask the students to transpose their running commentaries into a narrative style, writing the story (as they imagined it) in the past tense.

(B)   Ask the students to draw a plan of the area in which the 'story' takes place, labelling different places and objects. Then let them work in pairs and explain to one another why they drew the plan as they did.

17. ONE-SIDED TELEPHONE DIALOGUES

Level   Intermediate upwards

Outline

The recordings on the cassette each represent a telephone dialogue between two people, A and B. Only A, however, can be heard. It is left to the students to imagine what B is saying. They take the role of B and record what they think he or she is saying during A's pauses. They then swap booths to compare their classmates' versions.

Preparation

! (1)   There are two 'half-dialogues' on the cassette (See also page 71). Choose the one you want your students to do (the first is easier than the second).

(2)   Write this on the blackboard:

  A: Hello, I'd like to speak to Mr. Connolly, please.

  B: . . . .

  A: Oh, never mind, I'll call back later.

  B: . . . .

  A: I said: I'll call back later!

  B: . . . .

  A: Yes, that should be all right. Bye.

(3)   Ask the class to suggest what B is saying in this dialogue.

Procedure

(1)   Sit everyone in the lab and record one of the half-dialogues onto their tapes.

(2)   Explain to them what is written in **Outline** above.

(3)   Ask them to rewind and to record, in A's pauses, what they think B is saying (i.e. they take the part of B). Encourage them to go back and re-do parts where they made mistakes, where they hesitated too much, or where they didn't say enough to fill the gaps.

(4)   When they have all finished, ask them to swap booths with each other and compare results. Ask them especially to judge whether the dialogue 'sounds right', i.e. is it coherent?

Tapescript

Level   Lower intermediate upwards

The arrangement

Hello?

No, it's George.

Yes, it's about that. Listen: where are you going to get it?

I see. And who are you going to give it to?

Yes, but when are you going to see him?

Oh, I see. All right. Bye.

Tapescript

One-sided telephone dialogue No 2

Level   Intermediate upwards

An unexpected problem

Hello?

Yes, speaking.

Oh, hello! Sorry, I didn't recognise your voice.
How are things?

(*Gasp*!) No! really?

How did he manage to do that?

Knowing him, I can't say I'm surprised.
Remember what happened last time?

Yes, that's right! Anyway, what are we going to do about Saturday?

Yes, I suppose there's not much else we *can* do.

You're joking! That would cost a fortune!

Well, when can you let me know?

Okay, but not in the morning. I won't be in.

Bye!

18. OPEN DRILLS

Level   Intermediate upwards

Outline

In the lab, the students hear a series of comments made by different people. They must 'reply' to each comment with something they feel to be appropriate. Their replies, although having a degree of spontaneity, may each be required to contain a given pre-taught structure. An example of how different students might react to the same comment, using the same structure (here, 'must have (done something)'), is given below:

Comment: He's late again!

Possible   He must've missed his bus.

replies: He must've got up late.

He must've forgotten to come.

The students may subsequently swap booths to see how their classmates reacted.

Preparation

! (1)   Choose which of the open drills you want to use (see pages 75 and 76), then decide which structure (if any — you might choose to leave the drill *completely* open) you want it to be based on. Examples of structures you might choose are given here:

Open drill 1

Comment: Susan looks really tired today.

Possible   She *must've* been to a party last night.

structures   She *can't've* stayed up all night,

practised: surely?/*can* she?

Open drill 2

Comment: This cut on my hand has turned septic.

Possible   You *should've* put something on it!

structures   *Why didn't you* wash it properly?

practised: *If* you*'d* been more careful, it *wouldn't've* got infected!

Open drill 3

Comment: I don't know what's wrong with my car.

It keeps stalling.

Possible   *Have you tried* adjust*ing* the idling speed?
structures   *You'd better* check the petrol pump.
practised: *The trouble must be in* your carburettor.
             It sounds as if one of the jets is blocked.
             The spark plugs probably *need* clean*ing*.

! (2)   Pre-teach the structure(s) you have chosen. Also pre-teach any unknown vocabulary appearing in the drill. If you have chosen open drill 3, you will probably have to spend some time in the classroom introducing the 'car' vocabulary required in it (see next page).

Procedure

(1)   Sit the students in the lab and explain what they are to do (as in the first three sentences of **Outline**).

(2)   Record the chosen drill onto their tapes. (If your students are sufficiently advanced, let them speak their 'replies' onto their tapes at the same time).

(3)   Ask them to rewind and to record (or re-record) their replies.

(4)   Listen in and encourage them to re-record the corrections to any mistakes.

(5)   Now ask them to swap booths and compare how their classmates reacted to the comments. You can take advantage of this time to listen in again and jot down any mistakes you may have missed the first time. These can be dealt with later.

Development

Below is a list of 'replies'. Ask the students to supply as many of the preceding 'comments' as possible. This could be set as homework; results could be compared in the next lesson.

(a)   He must've been decorating.
(b)   Hmm. It sounds as if the points need changing.
(c)   You should've tried to dissuade him!
(d)   Why on earth didn't you change it?
(e)   If there hadn't been so many people, it would never've happened.
(f)   The battery probably wants charging.
(g)   She can't've finished already, can she?
(h)   Have you tried using sticky tape?
(i)   You'd better get rid of it before anyone finds out.
(j)   It sounds as if it isn't adjusted properly.

Vocabulary

Car vocabulary for open drill 3

For the driver
   ignition key
+ starter
+ choke (to pull the choke out)
+ accelerator (accelerator cable)
+ clutch (to let the clutch out)
+ brake (brake fluid; to
+   bleed the brakes; disc-
+   brake pads, brake linings)
+ handbrake (to take the hand
+   brake off)
   gear lever (to change gear;
     to change up/down
     gearbox)
   steering wheel (steering
     column)
   dashboard (speedometer;
+   odometer; fuel gauge;
+ battery gauge; temperature
     gauge)
   wing mirror; driving mirror
   windscreen wipers
+ headlights (full beam;
     dipped beam; to dip;
+ to dazzle)
   sidelights
   rear lights
+ brake lights
   reversing lights
   heated rear windscreen

The ignition
+ spark-plugs (high ten-
     sion leads)
+ distributor (distributor
+   head; points)
+ coil
+ dynamo/alternator

The cooling
+ radiator (radiator hose;
+   radiator cap; antifreeze)
+ water pump (to seize up)
+ fan (fan belt; tighten/loosen)
+ to overheat
+ to leak
+ to fur up

The engine
+ oil (oil level; dipstick;
+   oil filter)
+ to turn over (turn over
+   smoothly/irregularly)
+ revs (revolutions; r.p.m.;
+   high revs/low revs)
+ to stall
+ to judder
+ starter motor
+ tappets (camshaft)
   pistons (crankshaft)
+ valves
+ to tune the engine

Road holding
+ suspension
+ shock-absorbers
+ to corner (to corner badly)
+ to balance the wheels
+ tyres (tyre pressure; to pump up;
+   inner tube; tread;
+   worn)

Bodywork, etc.
   wing
   offside/nearside
   bonnet
   boot

+ battery (to charge the
+   battery; to top up the
+   battery; distilled water)

The fuel supply
+ carburettor (idling speed;
+   rich mixture; to tune
+   the carburettor; the jets)
+ petrol pump
+ fuel pipe (blockage)
+ air filter

    bumper
+ exhaust pipe (silencer)
+   paintwork (rust; to rub down;
+   to degrease; to prime; filler;
+   to respray; to wax)

Note: Only the items marked with a + are likely to be useful in the drill; the others have been included for the sake of completeness.

Tapescripts

'Open' drill 1

(1)   I wonder why Fred's limping like that.
(2)   Funny. I keep phoning George but there's no answer.
(3)   Have you seen that big dent in the manager's car?
(4)   He's late again!
(5)   I'm getting worried — Brian hasn't written for *ages.*
(6)   Hey, seen Peter lately? He's got a terrific black eye!
(7)   He's lost a lot of weight — I hardly recognised him.
(8)   Oh, damn! Where the hell did I put my keys?
(9)   Mmm! Carol looks very brown.
(10)   Hey — this letter isn't for us.
(11)   Oh, look — there's a note on our front door.
(12)   I don't understand — it's already eight o'clock and nobody's come yet.
(13)   Hey! What's happened? Why have all the lights gone out?
(14)   Susan looks really tired today.
(15)   Where the hell did all this water come from?

'Open' drill 2

(1)   I didn't like that film very much.
(2)   Oh, no! It's my wife's birthday today! I completely forgot!
(3)   Brr! It's much too cold here in Scotland!
(4)   I'm sorry — I've spilt my tea all over the carpet.
(5)   Yurgh! This cheap wine is bloody awful!
(6)   This cut on my hand has turned septic.
(7)   (Yawn)

(8)   My mother-in-law came last weekend. I had to stay in all the time.

(9)   Hey! I think we've taken the wrong turning.

(10) Would you believe it! My car's been stolen — *again!*

(11) Oooooooooh! I feel terrible.

(12) Hmm. Come to think of it, this suit *is* a bit small for me.

(13) I was bitten to death by those blasted mosquitoes last night!

(14) Oh, no, look at this! We're right in the middle of the rush-hour traffic!

(15) A - A - A - A - Atchooo!

'Open drill 3'

(1)   I don't know what's wrong with my car. It keeps stalling.

(2)   When I brake to slow down, it makes a horrible scraping noise.

(3)   When I've been driving for just a few minutes, the temperature gauge goes right up.

(4)   I had real trouble starting my car this morning.

(5)   It starts all right, but it turns over very irregularly.

(6)   My car has started making a hell of a noise.
      Everyone turns round when I drive past!

(7)   When I'm driving at high speed, the steering wheel vibrates.

(8)   I just can't get any acceleration out of my car any more.

(9)   Every time I go over a bump, it sounds as if the whole car is going to fall to pieces!

(10) I've no idea what's wrong — when I turn the ignition key, nothing happens.

(11) It starts all right, but when you accelerate, the engine just stops.

(12) I don't know why, but the brake pedal seems to be a bit soft lately.

(13) When I start the car moving, it makes a horrible juddering sound. Once it's moving, the juddering stops.

(14) I don't know why, but drivers on the other side of the road keep flashing me at night.

(15) It seems to be burning hell of a lot of petrol lately.

19. DO-IT-YOURSELF STORY KIT

Level   Upper-intermediate to advanced

Outline
You narrate a story to the class in the lab, recording it onto the students' tapes. At certain moments during the narration, you pause and invite the students to add parts to the story. You may, for example, ask them to describe a certain scene or character, or contribute to the storyline itself. You supply the 'skeleton' of the story and the students put the 'flesh' on it. Both your voice and the student's are recorded on each tape. At the end of the recording, the students swap booths to compare their classmates' versions with their own. They may, alternatively, stay in their booths to perfect their recordings.

Preparation
! (1)   Choose which of the two stories you are going to tell on pages 78 and 79).
! (2)   For this activity, the comprehension load should be minimal: explain any words in the skeleton story which are likely to cause problems.

Procedure
(1)   Start the machines so that both your voice and the student's voice can be recorded in each booth.
(2)   Read the 'skeleton' story; read it slowly and calmly so that the students don't feel too panicked when it's their turn to speak. During the pauses, listen to the general noise level of the students speaking, and begin the next part when it has dropped by about fifty per-cent.
(3)   When the recording is finished,
either: (a)   ask the student to swap booths and listen to each other's versions
or: (b)   ask them to rewind and re-do any parts they think they could improve on, and *then* swap.
(4)   Listen in from your console and jot down any noteworthy mistakes for correction later on.

Development
Ask the students to write out either their own version or that of a classmate. This could be set as homework to consolidate the corrections of the mistakes you noted earlier.

Do-it-yourself story 1

The shipwreck

Two hundred years ago, there was a young sailor called Thomas. He was an ordinary sailor on a big sailing ship going to India. What was his life like on the ship?

One hot afternoon, he and the other sailors weren't working. It was their rest period. Describe what the different sailors were doing.

Some clouds began to cover the sun. At first, they were only white and grey, but soon the sky was black. Soon after that, a terrible storm blew up. Describe the scene on the ship.

There was nothing they could do. The ship finally sank with everyone on it. Thomas managed to hold onto a piece of wood until morning came. When the sun rose, he could see land. He left the piece of wood and swam to the beach. How did he feel when he arrived?

Thomas slept for a long time. When he woke up, he walked around and discovered that he was on an island. Describe the island.

He also discovered that he was alone on the island. As he hadn't eaten for a long time, he began to feel very hungry. What did he do?

Later on in the afternoon, he saw a large object floating in the water. He decided to see what it was, so he swam out to get it. When he had brought it back to the beach, he discovered that it was a chest from the ship. He took a stone, broke the lock and opened it. What was inside?

Thomas knew he would be on the island for some time. He began to think about this. What did he decide to do?

One day, just as he was finishing his meal, he saw a ship coming. What happened next? Finish the story.

Tapescript

Do-it-yourself story 2

The woodcutter

Once upon a time, there was a woodcutter. He lived with his wife in a little cottage in the middle of a big forest. Although they both worked hard, they were very poor. Describe the inside of their cottage.

One morning, very early, before the birds had started singing, the woodcutter left the little cottage and went to cut some trees by the river. How did he feel as he walked through the forest that morning? When he reached the river, he started to cut a tree. The tree was very tall, and its wood was very hard. Suddenly, the axe slipped out of his hands and fell into the river. Why couldn't he get his axe back?

While he was standing sadly on the riverbank, the mysterious figure of a young girl slowly emerged from the river. Describe this mysterious girl.

The girl came out of the water and approached the woodcutter. What did they say to each other?

The girl went back into the river and disappeared into the water. A few moments later, she came up. She was holding a beautiful golden axe which shone in the morning sun. "Here's your axe!" she said. "That's a wonderful axe," said the woodcutter, "I've never seen one as beautiful as that, but it isn't mine". The girl put the golden axe on the bank and disappeared into the river a second time. The woodcutter waited on the bank. What happened next? Finish the story.

20. GET OUT OF THAT!

Level   Intermediate upwards

Outline
The students are put into the role of someone accused of suspicious or embarrassing behaviour (e.g. being late for their first interview, or being arrested with
a diamond necklace in their pocket). The students listen to their 'accusers' in
the lab and record their explanations in the gaps between each accusation. They
then swap booths to see how their classmates fared.

Preparation
 (1)   Look at the tapescripts on the following pages and decide what
        language (if any) you will need to pre-teach.
        Note: Situation 3 is obviously a man's role but could easily be played by
        a girl or woman (ask them to imagine what their boyfriends or husbands
        would say).
 (2)   Before the students go to the lab, divide the booths arbitrarily into three
        roughly equal listening groups.
 (3)   Record a different situation onto each group's tapes. (See
        PRACTICAL NOTES on page xiii).

Procedure
 (1)   Sit the students in the lab and explain what they will have to do (see
        Outline).
 (2)   Let them work at their own pace to complete the dialogues, rewinding
        to correct and asking you for help when necessary.
 (3)   When they have done this, ask them to swap booths to see how their
        classmates got on. Booth-swapping can of course be done:
        (a)   *within* listening groups, i.e. the students see how their neighbours
              dealt with the same situation.
        (b)   or *between* listening groups, i.e. they hear different situations.
 (4)   You can take advantage of this time to jot down any noteworthy
        mistakes to be dealt with later.

80

Tapescript

The Interview

Situation 1

You are at an important interview for a job. You discover that your interviewer already knows some embarrassing things about you. Be ready to give a good reason when he asks you to explain these things. You have about twenty seconds for each explanation.

> Good morning. Please sit down. Now, first of all, you can see that it's nine o'clock. The interview was for eight, or had you forgotten?
>
> All right, well never mind about that now. The important thing is you're here. Now, as you probably know, one of the requirements of this job is that you should be very presentable — well-dressed. When you came in, I noticed that your shoes were two different colours, one black, the other brown . . . Hmm . . .
>
> I see. While we're on the subject of appearance, perhaps you could explain about your hair . . .
>
> Hmm. I see. Well, let's have a look at your qualifications — yes — I see that you failed all your exams at school except astronomy. Do you perhaps plan to spend your working time here looking out of the window?
>
> All right, well we'll talk about that later. Now, the receptionist downstairs said that when you arrived, you took a fire extinguisher off the wall and squirted it all over her desk. What have you got to say about that?
>
> Aha. One final question. Can you please tell me why you have brought that dead fish to this interview?
>
> I see. Well, thank you very much. Don't ring us, we'll ring you.

Tapescript

The Suspect

Situation 2

You are being interrogated by the police in connection with a series of burglaries in the neighbourhood. They seem to have found a lot of evidence against you. Each time you're questioned about something, try to give a good reason. You have about twenty seconds for each explanation.

> Now, when we searched your flat the other day, we found a lot of money — ten thousand pounds — under the mattress of your bed. Now, that's rather strange, isn't it?
>
> I see . . . and another thing: your neighbour saw you leaving your flat

at three o'clock in the morning with a heavy bag. Were you . . . sleep-walking?

Oh, yes, and another thing: when we were searching your flat, we noticed you had four televisions. That's rather strange for someone who lives alone . . .

Aha. Perhaps you could also tell me what you were doing in Mrs. Pilkington's back garden at midnight last night . . .?

Now, these keys . . . there are sixty-seven keys here — all different sorts. Do you normally go out with so many keys in your pocket?

Hmm. And now we come to the most interesting little thing. Can you explain why this rather expensive-looking diamond necklace was found in your pocket when you were arrested? Hmm?

I hope the judge believes you. Okay, sergeant, cell three's empty, isn't it?

Tapescript

The suspicious wife

Situation 3

Your wife is obsessed with the idea that you're seeing another woman. Each time she asks you for an explanation for something, try to put her mind at rest. You have about twenty seconds for each explanation.

Darling, why were you home so late last night? It must've been about three o'clock when you finally came back.

Darling, (*sniff, sniff*) what's that smell of perfume on you? It's not mine.

And what's that red stuff on your collar? Looks like lipstick to me.

Oh, and another thing: who's 'Fifi'? I found a telephone number written on an envelope with 'Fifi' next to it.

What about this? Perhaps you could explain this bill from the Savoy hotel. I found it in your pocket. Champagne dinner for two — a hundred and twenty pounds. Who do you know who's worth so much?

I also found a long, blonde hair on your dinner jacket. Are you sure you're not keeping something from me, darling?

Well, if you want to know where I am, I'll be round at my mother's. Your dinner's in the oven.

21. MURDER AT THE MANOR

Level   Upper-intermediate to advanced

Outline

This is an activity for 7 or more students. Each student represents one of the suspects in a murder case. They are each given a role-sheet which outlines the character they are to represent and the individual evidence they have to offer.

Before going to the lab, the students are familiarised with the background elements of the situation in various lead-in activities in the class.

The 'suspects' sit in the lab and are 'interrogated' by the pre-recorded questions on the cassette; both the interrogation and the student's answers are recorded on each tape. When everyone has perfected their recorded answers, they swap booths and listen to the other suspects' evidence, trying to piece the information together into a solution to the mystery. The 'suspects' may then go back to the class to discuss their findings freely.

Preparation

!! (1)   Read through the news item (page 88), the role-sheets (pages 89 to 94) and the tapescripts (also page 94, the interrogation) to familiarise yourself with the story. Be ready to deal with any unknown language.

!! (2)   Decide how you are going to 'lead in' to this activity; some suggestions for preliminary class work are given here:

   (A) *Presentation of the news item*
      (i) Make a copy of the news item.
      (ii) Cut it up horizontally into its individual lines.
      (iii) Sit everyone in a circle and deal out the cut-up lines at random.
      (iv) Ask them to reconstruct the original text by *reading* their lines to each other.
          Students may not exchange lines or look at each other's: the sorting must be done *orally*.

   (B) *Presentation of the plan of the Manor*
      (i) Sit everyone in pairs, back-to-back with their partners.
      (ii) Give one student in each pair a copy of the plan.
      (iii) Each student with a plan must now explain to his or her partner how to draw it. Neither partner must peep at the other's paper.
      (iv) Let everyone compare results to see which pair produced the most accurate copies.

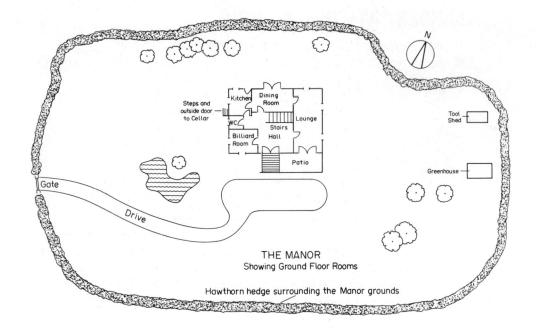

THE MANOR
Showing Ground Floor Rooms

Hawthorn hedge surrounding the Manor grounds

(C) *How to kill someone* (brainstorming)
  (i) Get the students to suggest how they would murder someone they hated.
 (ii) Ask what the advantages and disadvantages of each method would be.
(iii) Get them to think of as many *motives* for murder as possible.

(D) *Portraits*
  (i) Give each student the role-sheet he or she is to have in the lab later (see Procedure (2)).
 (ii) Ask each to draw a portrait of the character he or she is to play, on a separate piece of paper. (If your students aren't very artistic, use the portraits on the preceding pages).
(iii) Write the list of suspects on the board and fix the students' portraits near this with Blu-Tack.
 (iv) Now ask them to discuss which portraits match which suspects (no-one may mention his or her own portrait).

!! (3) Make sufficient copies of the 7 role-sheets to give each student one. (Although it doesn't matter if the number of students in the class is not divisible by 7, you will have to make sure that the role-sheets are distributed as evenly as possible, i.e. don't designate three butlers and only one Major, for example).

!! (4)   Make sufficient copies of the news item (page 88) and the plan of the Manor (page 84) to give each student one. Also make one copy of Inspector Nickham's evidence, page 95: (this will be needed during the lab phase).

Procedure

(1)   (*In the class*) Whatever lead-in activity you decide to do, make sure that everyone is familiar with:
   (a)   The essential details of the news item;
   (b)   The characters involved in the murder case;
   (c)   The plan of the Manor.

(2)   (*In the class*) Give each student a copy of one of the role-sheets. Let them choose their roles if you like, but make sure they are distributed evenly (see **Preparation** 3).

(3)   Sit the students in the lab with their role-sheets. Explain that they are now to assume the identity of the character outlined. Let them have 5–10 minutes to read silently and ask you any questions.

(4)   Explain that the police have a new method of interrogating suspects — in a language lab. Tell them to listen carefully and follow the instructions for the interrogation.

(5)   Broadcast the interrogation so that both the questions and the student's answers are recorded on each tape. The pauses between the questions are only very brief. Use the 'pause' or 'stop' facility on your console to lengthen the pauses appropriately.

(6)   At the end of the interrogation, let them work individually for a few minutes to correct and re-record their answers where necessary. You could listen in to provide individual guidance where required.

(7)   Now ask each of them to write the name of the character they played, in large letters, on a piece of paper; this will be left in the booth to show the future occupants whose evidence is recorded there.

(8)   Fix the copy of Inspector Nickham's evidence (page 95) to the wall with some Blu-Tack.

(9)   Ask the students to swap booths, listen to the other six suspects' evidence, and make notes. Later on during this phase, you may find that some students have to wait for certain booths to be vacated: ask them to have a look at Inspector Nickam's evidence on the wall, or encourage them to share and discuss their findings with each other, in the meantime. Some students may want to go back to previous booths to check details.

(10)   When you feel that the majority of students have heard enough, take everyone back to the classroom (or to a place where they can discuss).

(11) In small groups or as a class, ask them to share their findings and try to solve the mystery.

(12) If, after a reasonable time, no satisfactory solution is agreed upon, get the class to ask you questions with 'yes/no' answers to guide them towards the logical solution given below.

A logical solution to the murder mystery

Using his telephoto lens, the gardener, Ferdy Lazer, took a photo of Lord Rolling-Ennet and Laika Tagetemov in very compromising circumstances. He then blackmailed Lord Rolling-Ennet into giving him regular sums of money, threatening to show the photo to his wife, or sell it to a Sunday newspaper. Lord Rolling-Ennet was forced to pay up, and did so several times, but quietly contemplated his revenge. He formulated a brilliant plan — one which would not only rid him of his blackmailer, but also fulfil his dream of leaving the Manor, his boring, ugly wife, parasitic son and daughter-in-law, and enable him to fly off to Miami with Laika.

One day, he look Lazer down to the cellar on the pretext of showing him some alterations he wanted doing there. He then hit Lazer over the head with a shovel, killing him. Next, he put Lazer's clothes on, stuffed the body and his own clothes into the big boiler, and burnt everything. He emerged from the cellar, in Lazer's clothes, just as Smarming was coming down into it. He had to cover his face with a handkerchief and avoid speaking in case Smarming recognised him. He then went off to hide in a secluded part of the garden, in case anyone else approached him. He waited until 6.20 to leave the Manor, the time when Lazer normally went off to the pub. At this time, he took Lazer's bike and went off, but as he was not used to riding bicycles, he wobbled about a lot, and even fell off.

His plan was to hide out until the will had been read: Laika was one of the beneficiaries. She would then rejoin him and they would fly off to Miami together.

He realised that the almost completely burnt body in the boiler could only be identified by a dentist, who would be able to recognise his work on one of his own patient's teeth.

The police would automatically assume that the body was Lord Rolling-Ennet's, and call in Mr. Nash, his dentist, to identify it. Lord Rolling-Ennet therefore took the precaution of bribing Mr. Nash (very generously) to say that the body *was* his.

Other evidence which he rigged, to incriminate Lazer, included sending himself an anonymous threatening letter, made of cut-up newspapers; the remains of these newspapers (the *Garden Gazette*) were planted in the greenhouse.

Development

If this, or another acceptable solution, is arrived at, ask the students to write a second newspaper report explaining it.

EVENING SUN

LORD ROLLING-ENNET MURDERED

CHARRED BODY FOUND IN BASEMENT BOILER

Lord Mussbeigh Rolling-Ennet, the millionaire race-horse owner and chairman of the Rolling-Ennet carpet industry, has been murdered at his country home near Bargum, Southumberland.

Police, following up Lady Rolling-Ennet's call that her husband had gone missing, found the charred remains of the 55-year-old nobleman in the basement boiler of the manor after a routine search last night.

The police are certain that whoever is responsible for the murder was anxious to destroy the body, since the way in which Lord Rolling-Ennet died could well provide a clue to the killer's identity.

The body was, in fact, so badly burned that it could only be identified by Lord Rolling-Ennet's dentist, Mr. Nash, who was able to recognise his work on the dead man's teeth.

Ferdy Lazer, 44, the gardener at the manor, has not been seen since the day of the murder, and is being sought by the police to help in their enquiries.

Lazer is believed to be wearing a black hat and blue dungarees; Scotland Yard have appealed to anyone who has seen a man fitting this description to contact them.

Lady Hyma Rolling-Ennet

Married Lord Mussbeigh Rolling-Ennet in 1945. Only son, Simon, engaged to Orma Gould. Disappointed: not right girl for Simon — *common* family — only interested in our money. Mussbeigh invited Laika Tagetemov, Russian dancer, to stay at Manor. Still here *now*! Young, attractive, lively. Mussbeigh and I — not on good terms lately — Mussbeigh too busy with Laika to bother with his own wife. Mussbeigh wrote new will in August — did not reveal details.

1.30	Lunch. Laika not as talkative as usual. Strange. Usually dominates conversation.
3.00	Go to bedroom — do some embroidery. Notice my embroidery scissors *missing* from needlework box.
3.30	Too tired for embroidery — have afternoon nap on bed.
4.30	Wake up — go downstairs. Find Simon + Orma playing scrabble. Not very interesting for Simon: Orma very ignorant and uncultured — no vocabulary. I join in next game — more interesting for Simon.
4.45	Smarming brings tea + cakes.
5.30	Game over. Too tired for another. Go to lounge alone. Watch film: *The Magnificent Seven.*
7.45	Wake up in armchair — film already finished. Smarming enters — asks if Lord R.-E. having dinner (funny question). I say "Yes, why?" — replies "Lord R.-E. not in house". I find others in hall — look confused. Simon says gardener gone *too*! Worried — phone police.
8.25	Police arrive — dogs — search everywhere.
8.45	Find Mussbeigh in cellar . . .

Simon Rolling-Ennet (36)

Lord + Lady Rolling-Ennet's only son. Engaged to Orma Gould, 22. Marry June next year. Parents don't approve: Orma's father only a bus-conductor. This attitude makes me extremely angry. Delicate problem in household recently: father sacked gardener + old-job man, Arthur Mow: 'indiscreet behaviour'. But Ida Down (maid + cook) *in love* with Mow (often saw them in garden together). Probably hated father for this.

1.30   Lunch.
3.30   Go to library to get Scrabble while Smarming clears table.
4.10   Begin Scrabble game. Orma useless! Takes 10 minutes to make 1 word!
4.30   Mother enters — joins in 2nd game.
4.45   Smarming enters — serves tea — we continue.
5.30   Mother goes next door to see film.
5.45   T.V. too loud — we give up 3rd game. Decide to go out into garden. See Major looking at something on lawn: dead mole — Major says he shot it with army revolver. Orma not impressed. Nice afternoon — we decide to walk to village — get cigarettes.
6.00   Pass Mr. Nash's house (our dentist). Surprised — see expensive sports car (Porsche!) parked in drive — 'FOR SALE' sign on house(!?)
6.30   On way back from town — see gardener (Lazer) on bike (opposite direction). Seems in a hurry — didn't even say 'good afternoon'.
6.40   We arrive back at Manor. Major + Laika on patio — drinking whisky. Major excited — telling old army story (I've heard it twice before). Orma stops to listen — I go to practise billiards.
7.00   Major comes in billiard room — we have game together. Major not on form.
7.45   I win (Major: too much whisky). Decide to invite father to play before dinner. Can't find him — look upstairs — in garden — nowhere.
8.00   Family realises Lord R.-E. missing. Mother very anxious — telephones police.

Orma Gould (22)

Future daughter-in-law of Rolling-Ennets. Engaged to Simon: wonderful man, but parents terribly snobbish — give me impression I'm not good enough for them — probably wanted upper-class wife for *their* son! Came to stay at Manor in August. Parents: always cold reception but Major + Laika O.K. — friendly. Remember last week, Simon looking for me in garden. Decided to play joke on him — hid behind greenhouse. Noticed Lord R.-E. and gardener (Lazer) *inside*. They couldn't see me. Lord R.-E. looked *furious*! Saw him give money to Lazer. I didn't tell others — too frightened.

1.30	Lunch. Fish (no chips). Simon eats Lord R.-E.'s. fish (greedy pig) — Lord R.-E. not very hungry.
3.00	Simon suggests Scrabble game. Hate Scrabble, but agree — nothing else to do. We get Scrabble box — wait for butler to finish in dining room — start game on table.
4.30	Lady R.-E. pokes her nose into our game — decides to play. We begin new game. I stay to be polite.
5.30	End of game. Lady R.-E. goes off somewhere — hear T.V. blaring in next room (old girl must be a bit deaf!). Can't play Scrabble any more — too much noise.
5.45	We go out into garden. See Major looking at something on lawn — dead mole (!) — says he *shot* it! Poor little thing! Simon in need of fags — suggests we walk to town.
6.30	Coming back from town — see gardener on bike (recognise ridiculous black hat). We say 'good afternoon' — no reply (ignorant pig). Can't ride bike very well. either!
6.45	Back at Manor. Major in garden with Laika. Major telling War story — I stop to listen — Simon goes to play billiards.
7.00	Major goes to see Simon. I stay with Laika — shows me photos — family, ballet etc.
7.15	Getting dark — we go to drawing room. I tell Laika about gardener on bike. She goes very red — hateful expression on face — says gardener 'horrible character' — didn't say why. Seemed embarrassed — changed subject.
8.00	Big fuss — Lord R.-E. missing. Lady R.-E. phones police.

Major Minedupp (54)

Old friend of Mussbeigh's — (school, army, etc.). Russian girl (Laika) also staying at Manor — pretty, fun-loving, etc. Exact opposite of Lady Hyma. Some friction: Mussbeigh spends more time with Laika. Mussbeigh depressed recently — told me: "fed up with life at Manor — too much responsibility — need change — money not everything," etc., etc.

1.30	Lunch. Tense atmosphere (like before battle).
3.00	Decide to sit in garden. Laika comes out later in bikini (lovely girl) — sunbathes on lawn (not much sun in Moscow).
3.15	Feel sleepy (heavy lunch) — decide to walk round gardens. Nice day. Pass Mussbeigh + gardener in back garden — talking about "modifications to cellar" — seem busy so I continue.
3.30	Begin to feel effects of wine + coffee — nobody looking — in bushes quickly.
3.45	Back to house — sit on patio — do *Times* crossword. Laika asleep on grass (difficult to concentrate!).
4.30	Laika wakes up — goes in. Comes back later (dressed). We chat — charming girl — wish I was young! Tea served.
5.10	Laika goes indoors. Suddenly, I see mole making terrible hole in beautiful lawn — I go up to get revolver! Come back down — wait for little devil — must be patient.
5.45	Moles pops us (at last!) — I get him with 2nd shot — go to inspect. Simon + Orma appear — Orma doesn't appreciate dead mole. They go off to village together. I sit on patio — finish crossword — call Smarming for whisky.
6.00	Laika joins me — we chat some more.
6.20	Notice gardener going out of front gate on bike — seems to have trouble with bike — falls off.
6.45	Simon + Orma come back from village. Simon goes in (billiards) — Orma stays to chat on patio.
7.00	Decide to teach Simon how to play! Leave girls on patio.
7.45	Simon suggests we ask Mussbeigh to play — we look for him. Can't find him. Upstairs? No. (??).
8.00	Downstairs in hall — everyone puzzled — no-one seen him. Lady Hyma very worried — rings police.

Laika Tagetemov (35)

Guest at Rolling-Ennets'. Russian ballet dancer. Lord Mussbeigh: a ballet fanatic. Invited me to stay at Manor. Charming man, good taste, culture, education, etc. *Boring* wife, Lady Hyma Rolling-Ennet: sleeps all day — probably jealous of me.

1.30	Lunch.
3.00	Lunch over. Lady R.-E. disappears upstairs. Simon suggests Scrabble game — I'm not interested — nice day — prefer to sit in sun. I go upstairs to change (bikini).
3.10	Sunbathe in garden. Major goes for walk round garden.
3.50	Notice gardener (Ferdy Lazer) crossing garden. He thinks I'm asleep. See him disappear into trees behind greenhouse (?). Sun nice and hot — I sleep.
4.30	I wake up (getting a bit cold) decide to get dressed. Pass Major on patio — doing crossword. Pass Lady R.-E. on stairs (looks at me coldly) — something *evil* about that woman.
4.45	Back to patio — tea + cakes with Major. We chat.
5.10	Major goes upstairs.
5.15	I decide to practise flute. Upstairs to get it. Pass Major coming down.
5.20	Start practising flute (drawing room).
6.00	Take flute back upstairs. Loud music coming from lounge (?). Back to patio — major sitting there drinking whisky. Tells me old soldier's stories.
6.45	Simon + Orma come in front gate. Orma sits down with us — Simon goes in.
7.00	Major goes in. I show Orma some photos. Getting cold, so we go into drawing room. We chat about cooking, etc.
7.45	Simon comes in — asks after Mussbeigh — we have no idea where he is.
8.00	Lady R.-E. rings police — *pretends* to be hysterical (good actress).

Smarming (65)

Rolling-Ennets' butler since 1956. Duties: organising meals, reception + staff (Ida Down, maid + cook; Ferdy Lazer, gardener + old-job man). previous gardener (Arthur Mow) sacked — sordid affair — improper advances to Ida Down. My duty to report this to Lord R.-E.: Lord R.-E.: real gentleman — pleasure to serve. Son, Simon, in pharmaceutical business — doing very badly — money problems. *Not* like his father.

1.30	I serve dinner.
3.00	Clear table. Trip over something on floor — drop tray of glasses (expensive crystal — hope no-one notices).
3.15	Clean kitchen.
3.45	Go down to cellar to get wine (dinner tonight). Pass Lazer on stairs. Remind him about lighting boiler (must have plenty of hot water) — says nothing — nods. Seems in a hurry — wiping face with handkerchief — hot in cellar. Wearing black hat — strange — usually takes it off indoors (?). In cellar, notice boiler already lit. Select wine — go upstairs to kitchen.
3.50	Afternoon tea for Lazer, Down + me. Lazer away somewhere — his tea gets cold. Relax till 4.30
4.30	Down prepares tea for family + guests — I serve — back to kitchen for cakes. Notice Down has distinctly guilty look on face (??)
4.50	Go to greenhouse to get tomatoes (tonight's salad). Notice pile of newspapers (*Garden Gazette*) in corner. Seem damaged — rats again? Back to kitchen — another rest before dinner preparations. Notice Down asleep outside.
5.45	Hear bangs (Major's old car?).
6.00	Begin dinner preparations.
7.00	Preparations finished — lay table.
7.30	Simon R.-E. asks me: 'seen father?' — I say no. Decide to look for him — everywhere — Lord R.-E. gone.
7.45	I ask Lady R.-E. if Lord R.-E. dining tonight. She seems surprised. I say Lord R.-E. gone out somewhere — not in house. Lady R.-E. very worried — phones police.

Ida Down (33)

Maid + cook at Manor. Started 3 years ago. *Not* very well paid. Arthur Mow (gardener) started just after me. Sacked 2 months ago (don't know why). New gardener + odd-job man: Ferdy Lazer. Butler: Smarming (can't stand him! Snobbish, old-fashioned, etc.). When cleaning Miss Tagetemov's room last week, noticed two air tickets (Miami!) in drawer. Also overheard angry conversation between Simon + Lord R.-E. in billiard room — distinctly remember Simon saying: "It's not just for the money". (Now that Lord R.-E. dead, Simon very rich).

1.30	In kitchen — seeing to lunch for family + guests.
3.00	Washing-up (Strange — not many glasses). Noticed Smarming's face — unusually red (?).
3.20	Through kitchen window, see Ferdy (new gardener) talking to Lord R.-E. in back garden — approaching house.
3.30	Notice Major at end of garden. Looks round make sure no-one looking — suddenly disappears into small trees — comes out a minute later (??) — walks off towards greenhouse.
3.45	Smarming goes out. I make afternoon tea for Ferdy, me + Smarming.
3.50	Smarming comes back with bottles. Ferdy doesn't come — tea alone with Smarming (embarrassing silence!). Have rest till 4.30 — lot of work to do later.
4.30	Make tea for family + guests. Smarming takes it out — forgets to take cakes in pantry — feel hungry — I pinch a cake quickly — won't notice. Another one? Too late! Smarming back. He goes off with cakes.
5.00	Smarming comes back with tomatoes. I relax in kitchen garden till 6. Smarming listens to football results in kitchen (strange for someone so snobbish).
5.45	Hear bangs (Ferdy doing odd-jobs) — wakes me up.
6.00	Begin dinner preparations — non stop till 7.15.
6.20	Ferdy goes off to village pub on bike (as usual) — see him through window. Looks very wobbly on bike today — drunk already?
7.15	Dinner finished — clean kitchen — Smarming helps (or pretends to!).
8.00	Hear excited talking in hall (not *another* guest. I hope — two already more than enough!

Tapescript

Interrogation

Good afternoon. This is Inspector Nickham of Scotland Yard. Thank you for accepting to come here today. As you probably know, police methods have been modernised recently. In a few moments, you'll be asked to give some information. This information will be processed by a computer, so please speak clearly and concisely with a minimum of hesitation.

The answers to the following questions are of utmost importance in this case: please answer them as fully as possible. You are warned that your recording will be tested with a lie-detector. Please be ready for the first question.

Question one: What's your name?

Question two: What relationship did you have to Lord Rolling-Ennet?

Question three: Did you ever see anyone at the Manor act in a suspicious or unusual way? Think carefully, now.

Question four: What were *your* feelings towards Lord Rolling-Ennet?

Question five: What were you doing at exactly 5.45 the day of the murder? Did you hear anything strange?

Question six: Do you know of any reason, however insignificant it may seem to you, why anyone should want to kill Lord Rolling-Ennet?

Question seven: This is the last question. Have you got any other evidence which might be helpful in this case? Remember: insignificant things can sometimes be important.

Inspector Nickham

Summary of evidence found by police

(1) Ferdy Lazer, gardener at Manor, disappeared day of murder.

(2) Police sergeant reports seeing Lazer in pub last week — buying drinks for everyone — said he won money on horses.

(3) Lady Rolling-Ennet found letter (made of cut-up newspapers) threatening Lord R.-E. Lord R.-E. did not take it very seriously. Remains of newspapers found in greenhouse.

(4) Loaded gun *with 2 rounds missing* found in Major Minedupp's room.

(5) Traces of *blood* on floor in dining room.

(6) Smarming's silver pen found in cellar.

(7) Lord Rolling-Ennet's will changed recently — now in favour of Laika Tagetemov, friend and guest of Rolling-Ennets.

(8) Lazer's room searched — found camera + telephoto lens. Nobody at Manor knew Lazer was photographer — strange.

List of people involved in the case

      Lord Mussbeigh Rolling-Ennet

*   Lady Hyma Rolling-Ennet (wife of deceased)

*   Simon Rolling-Ennet (Rolling-Ennet's only son)

*   Orma Gould (Simon's financée)

*   Major Minedupp (friend and guest of Lord Rolling-Ennet)

*   Laika Tagetemov (friend and guest of Lord Rolling-Ennet)

*   Smarming (butler at the Manor)

*   Ida Down (maid and cook at the Manor)

      Arthur Mow (former gardener and odd-job man at the Manor)

      Ferdy Lazer (new gardener and odd-job man at the Manor)

      Mr. Nash (Lord Rolling-Ennet's dentist (identified body))

* = suspects available for interrogation

22. TELL THE STORY YOUR WAY

Level   Lower-intermediate upwards

Outline
The students listen to a short, pre-recorded story in their booths at their own speed. They then re-tell it in their own words on an erased portion of tape. By listening again, they are more aware of the shortcomings of their first versions, and are in a better position to re-record an improved second one.

Preparation
! (1)   There are two short stories recorded on the cassette. As the first is simpler than the second, it might be a good idea to start with this one; check by listening.
! (2)   Erase about ten minutes of tape in the student's booths (see **Practical notes** on page xiii).
! (3)   Record one of the short stories onto the student's tapes at the beginning of the erased portion. There should be about six or seven minutes of blank tape after the recorded story.

Procedure
(1)   Sit the students in the lab and let them listen at their own speed to the recorded story. The basic story must be understood by everyone so encourage them to ask questions when necessary.
(2)   When they have had sufficient time to listen, ask them to wind *to the end* of the recorded story.
(3)   Now ask them, working individually, to record the story in their own words onto the blank portions of tape. They should not, during this phase, wind back to listen to the original story.
(4)   Listen in discreetly to different students and make a note of all the commoner mistakes you hear.
(5)   When everyone has finished, bring up the mistakes you noted and invite corrections from the class.
(6)   Now ask them to rewind to the end of original story and to re-record a second version, paying particular attention to the mistakes you have just dealt with.
(7)   Again, listen in and jot down the commoner mistakes.
(8)   Invite corrections to these mistakes when everyone has finished.

Development
Ask the students to write out the story. This could easily be set as homework to consolidate the points you brought up during the correction phases.

Tapescript

A Desert Story

Level Lower intermediate

A man was lost in the desert. He was very thirsty and very tired. The sun was hot. After two hours in the desert, he saw an Arab on a camel. He went to the Arab and said: "Water! Water! I must have some water! Have you got any water, please?"

"I'm sorry," said the Arab, "I haven't got any water, but look! I've got some beautiful ties! Which colour would you like? Blue? Green? Red? Yellow, perhaps?"

"I don't want any ties!" said the man, "I want some water!"

"I'm sorry," said the Arab, "I haven't got any," and he went away.

After three hours in the desert, the man saw a second Arab. "Water! Water! I must have some water! *Please* give me some water!"

"I'm sorry," said the Arab, "I haven't got any. But how about a nice, smart tie? Would you like this nice blue one, or would you prefer a black one?"

"I don't want a tie!" replied the poor man. "I only want some water!"

"Oh, I'm sorry," Said the Arab, "I've only got ties."

After four hours in the desert, the man was very, very thirsty and very, very tired. Suddenly, he saw a big hotel in the distance. "Is it a mirage?" he thought. "No! It isn't! It's a hotel! I'm saved!" He went to the hotel and there was a man by the door. "Water! Water! he said to the doorman, I'm very thirsty. Can I come in and have some water, please?"

"I'm very sorry, sir . . ." said the doorman.

"Haven't you got any water?" asked the surprised man.

"We've got plenty of water," he replied, "but you can't come in. You haven't got a tie."

Tapescript

The King of the Frogs

Level Intermediate upwards

Many years ago, before there were any men on the Earth, there was an immense forest. There were all kinds of animals roaming the forest, and there was also a huge lake, which was the home of many frogs.

Now, in those days, frogs used to make a terrible noise, croaking all through the day and night. In fact there was so much noise in the lake that some of the frogs decided it was time to put a stop to it. "We need a king." they said. "A king will command so much respect that no-one will dare make a noise any more."

They decided to go and see their god, Buni, on the other side of the lake. "O great Buni," said one of the frogs, "we want a king." Now, although Buni was a hundred times the size of an ordinary frog, he was very lazy, and couldn't be bothered to find a real king for the frogs. "So, you want a king?" he said. "All right, I'll give you a king." Then, he picked up a big stone and threw it into the middle of the lake. It landed with a terrible splash, and immediately all the frogs stopped croaking. They could all see the stone in the middle of the lake. None of them dared to croak, or go near it, because they thought it was their king.

After a few days, however, some of the frogs began to feel a little braver. they swam nearer and nearer the stone to have a closer look at their king. Then, one day, one of the frogs went right up to the stone and actually touched it. "This isn't a king!" he shouted to the other frogs, "It's just a stone!"

When the other frogs realised that their king was nothing more than a stone, they were very angry with Buni for making such fools of them. They went back to the other side of the lake to see their god. "We asked you for a king!" they shouted, "And all you gave us was a stone!" Buni started to get angry too. He was tired of these annoying little frogs disturbing his peace. "All right!" he boomed in a terrible voice, "If you want a real king, I'll give you one this time!" Buni then took another stone and hurled it into the middle of the lake. As soon as it touched the water, it turned into a crocodile.

Some of the frogs didn't believe it was their king; they thought that Buni had tried to fool them with another stone. They went up to the crocodile and touched it. Suddenly, it opened its huge mouth and the frogs could see its awful yellow teeth glinting in the sun. They were terrified of their new king, and swam away to hide. Then, the crocodile began to swim round the lake. The frogs were scared. If they croaked, the crocodile would know where to find them, and come and eat them.

From that day onward, the only time the frogs dared to croak was at night, when the crocodile was asleep. That's why, today, frogs only croak at night. But if you throw a stone into the water, they'll stop croaking for a long time. They think Buni is sending them an even more terrible king.